# JOHN MARSHALL AND INTERNATIONAL LAW

**Recent Titles in**
**Contributions in Political Science**

Power and Civil Society: Toward a Dynamic Theory of Real Socialism
*Leszek Nowak*

Public Policy and the Public Good
*Ethan Fishman, editor*

The U.S. Consul at Work
*William D. Morgan and Charles Stuart Kennedy*

Reluctant Ally: United States Foreign Policy Toward the Jews from Wilson to Roosevelt
*Frank W. Brecher*

Ethics for Public Managers
*Harold F. Gortner*

Power and Service: A Cross-National Analysis of Public Administration
*Hardy Wickwar*

Richard M. Nixon: Politician, President, Administrator
*Leon Friedman and William F. Levantrosser, editors*

Gubernatorial Leadership and State Policy
*Eric B. Herzik and Brent W. Brown, editors*

The West European Allies, the Third World, and U.S. Policy: Post–Cold War Challenges
*Richard J. Payne*

Political Participation and American Democracy
*William Crotty, editor*

The Federalists, the Antifederalists, and the American Political Tradition
*Wilson Carey McWilliams and Michael T. Gibbons, editors*

Public Policy Issues in Wildlife Management
*William R. Mangun, editor*

Israeli Politics in the 1990s: Key Domestic and Foreign Policy Factors
*Bernard Reich and Gershon R. Kieval, editors*

# JOHN MARSHALL AND INTERNATIONAL LAW

## Statesman and Chief Justice

Frances Howell Rudko

Contributions in Political Science, Number 280
*Bernard K. Johnpoll, Series Editor*

GREENWOOD PRESS
New York • Westport, Connecticut • London

**Library of Congress Cataloging-in-Publication Data**

Rudko, Frances Howell
John Marshall and international law : statesman and Chief Justice / Frances Howell Rudko.
p. cm.—(Contributions in political science, ISSN 0147-1066 ; no. 280)
Includes bibliographical references and index.
ISBN 0-313-27932-2 (alk. paper)
1. Marshall, John, 1755-1835. 2. Statesmen—United States—Biography. 3. Judges—United States—Biography. 4. United States—Foreign relations—1789-1797. 5. United States—Foreign relations—1797-1801. I. Title. II. Series.
E302.6.M4R83 1991
347.73'2634—dc20
[347.3073534] 91-11333

British Library Cataloguing in Publication Data is available.



Library of Congress Catalog Card Number: 91-11333
ISBN: 0-313-27932-2
ISSN: 0147-1066

First published in 1991

Greenwood Press, 88 Post Road West, Westport, CT 06881
An imprint of Greenwood Publishing Group, Inc.

Printed in the United States of America

The paper used in this book complies with the Permanent Paper Standard issued by the National Information Standards Organization (Z39.48-1984).

10 9 8 7 6 5 4 3 2 1

For My Sons,
Michael, Stephen, and
Gregory

However preeminent the ancients may have been in some of the fine arts, they were, I think you very clearly show, much inferior to us, or a great way behind us, in the more solid & more interesting principles of international law; —— a law which contributes more to the happiness of the human race than all the statues which ever came from the hands of the sculptor, or all the paintings that were ever placed on canvass. I do not, by this, mean to lessen the value of the arts. I subscribe to their importance, & admit that they improve as well as embellish human life & manners; but they yield in magnitude to those moral rules which regulate the communion of man with man.

John Marshall to Henry Wheaton, March 24, 1821, on Wheaton's book—
*A Digest of the Law of Maritime Captures*,
The Pierpont Morgan Library, New York, MA 995.

# Contents

# Acknowledgments

For the preparation of this work, I am indebted to the staffs of the law libraries at The Ohio State University School of Law in Columbus, Ohio, and the University of Arkansas School of Law in Fayetteville, Arkansas, and to the librarians of the William Oxley Thompson Library at The Ohio State University and the Mullins Library at the University of Arkansas. Archivists of the Virginia State Library and the Virginia Historical Society in Richmond, Virginia, the Earl Gregg Swem Library of The College of William and Mary in Williamsburg, Virginia, the National Archives and the Library of Congress in Washington, D.C., and The Pierpont Morgan Library in New York City were especially helpful. Professors James S. Chase and Willard B. Gatewood of the History Department at the University of Arkansas read and made valuable suggestions as did the editorial personnel at Greenwood Press. Mildred Vasan and Catherine Lyons of Greenwood Press deserve special thanks as does Rebecca Bennett of New York City who contributed so much to the final form of the manuscript.

Scholarly interest in the history of international law has been intense during certain periods, and significant publications have appeared sporadically since the late eighteenth century. I am indebted to this scholarship and have noted it throughout the text. The exploration of this fascinating aspect of the work of John Marshall was also enhanced by exhaustive current volumes. The editors of *The Papers of John Marshall* and the authors of the Marshall era in the *Oliver Wendell Holmes Devise History of the Supreme Court* contributed immeasurably to meaningful study, as did the excellent research facilities at The Ohio State University.

# 1
# Introduction

John Marshall became Chief Justice of the Supreme Court in 1801 at the age of forty-six. During his thirty-five year tenure (1801-1835), he wrote opinions in approximately eighty cases involving international law.[1] Unquestionably until eight years before his appointment, Marshall's view of the world was largely insular. Only in 1793 did he begin to focus on international problems and to work toward resolving them through the application of international law. Most scholars who have considered the question contend that Marshall learned international law from counsels' arguments in cases which came before the Court and that his decisions reflect primarily on-the-job training. However, a close analysis of his experiences between 1793 and 1801, considered in relation to his decisions on international law while on the Court, reveals not only that he was schooled intensively in international law before he became Chief Justice, but also that he later applied the principles learned during his earlier experiences.

Marshall's immediate background was certainly parochial. He was born amid frontier conditions on September 24, 1755, at Germantown in Fauquier County, Virginia, the first of fifteen children born to Mary Randolph Keith Marshall and Thomas Marshall. Thomas Marshall, a surveyor, land speculator, and planter, participated fully in the political life of the county, colony, and state. He worked to improve his condition and, by the time he moved west to Kentucky in 1783, his estate of several thousand acres and twenty slaves was the largest in the county. While in Virginia, he served as Fauquier County surveyor, justice of the peace and sheriff, and as a representative in the House of Burgesses from 1761 to 1775. He personally supervised John Marshall's early education, instilling in him a love for history and poetry. Formal schooling, however, was brief, comprising only one year of study at Archibald Campbell's Academy in 1769. The following year, a Scottish minister, James Thomson, was sent from Edinburgh, Scotland to serve the local parish; at Thomas Marshall's request, he lived with the Marshall family, tutoring the children in Greek and Latin. During this period, young Marshall began to read Horace and Livy.[2] Among the books in Thomas Marshall's small library was a four-volume set of Sir William Blackstone's *Commentaries on the Laws of England* which introduced John Marshall to the law.[3]

A lifelong personal friend to George Washington, Thomas Marshall served under him during the Revolution, as did his sons. Thomas Marshall organized the militia in Fauquier County in 1775, served with the rank of major in the Culpeper Minutemen Battallion and, subsequently, as major and colonel in the Continental Army. John Marshall, like his father, served both in the militia, including the Culpeper Minutemen Battallion, and in the Continental Army as first lieutenant, Virginia Continental Line, llth Virginia Regiment. With his father and two of his brothers, Marshall endured the harsh winter at Valley Forge, where he experienced first hand the inefficiency of the weak Continental Congress. This experience may have, as his biographer Albert Beveridge suggests, committed him to a strongly national form of union.[4] John Marshall also saw action at the battles of Brandywine Creek, Germantown, and at Monmouth Courthouse.[5]

After the Revolution, Marshall briefly attended lectures at The College of William and Mary given by the celebrated professor of law and patriot, George Wythe.[6] Practicing law initially in 1780 in Fauquier County,[7] Marshall moved his practice in 1783 to Richmond, when he married Mary "Polly" Ambler, the second daughter of Rebecca Burwell Ambler and Jaquelin Ambler, state treasurer.

Marshall's political awareness until 1793 was conditioned by local and state issues. He was first elected to the lower house of the Virginia legislature in 1782 and he served virtually consecutive terms thereafter, representing initially Fauquier County and, after 1787, Henrico County.[8] This experience critically shaped Marshall's views, as he later professed "the general tendency of state politics convinced me that no safe and permanent remedy could be found but in a more efficient and better organized general government."[9] Chosen as delegate to the Constitutional ratification convention which met in Richmond, June 2-27, 1788, Marshall, already impressed by the need for a strong national government, energetically advocated the adoption of the Constitution. He delivered speeches at the convention dealing with three aspects of the new Constitution, general distribution of powers, control and training of the militia, and the formation of the judiciary.[10]

Marshall's interest in politics increased in 1792 with the advent of war between revolutionary France and the monarchical powers, chiefly England. Already a staunch supporter of Washington, he became a strong apologist for the foreign policy embraced by the administration. Events following the Proclamation of Neutrality on April 22, 1793, ushered Marshall into the national political arena.

In a relatively brief period of eight years, Marshall argued before the Supreme Court as debtors' counsel in the test case against pre-Revolutionary British creditors, represented his nation's interests in a critical diplomatic mission to France, served in the House of Representatives, and directed the foreign policy of the United States as Secretary of State. The following study focuses on these four events in his life as they provided the foundation for his understanding of the principles of international law that he later articulated on the Supreme Court.

Marshall applied legal rules, principles, and concepts of the law of nations that he learned during what amounted to an eight-year apprenticeship. The historian Alexander DeConde wrote that the Federalists left the "center of the national stage with the nation's major grievances in foreign affairs settled."[11] As the last Federalist Secretary of State, Marshall certainly left center stage, but he merely moved backstage to continue learning and to decide issues, using principles that he had previously defined. The Constitution referred to the law of nations, and it was initially accepted into the law of the land.[12] Marshall did not hesitate to define international law as rigorously as he enunciated more conventional constitutional principles.

Chancellor James Kent of New York, distinquished jurist and professor of law at Columbia College, described in 1826 the significance of the law of nations to the United States, observing, in words that reflected Marshall's understanding, that:

> When the United States ceased to be a part of the British empire, and assumed the character of an independent nation, they became subject to that system of rules which reason, morality, and custom had established among the civilized nations of Europe, as their public law. During the war of the American revolution, Congress claimed cognizance of all matters arising upon the law of nations, and they professed obedience to that law, "according to the general usages of Europe." By this law we are to understand that code of public instruction, which defines the rights and prescribes the duties of nations, in their intercourse with each other. The faithful observance of this law is essential to national character, and to the happiness of mankind.[13]

Between 1793 and 1801 when Marshall served the nation in an international context, he worked on a daily basis with the realities of international relations, and was schooled in the specifics of international law. He was particularly suited to deal with the organic nature of international law, which required creative logic and application of basic principles to the contemporary political situation. The principles of international law developed and applied during the period were influenced not only by the foreign policy of the United States assuming its place in the world but also by the relative power positions held by the European countries in the international community. Unlike the law specifically expressed in statutes and in constitutions, international law was to be carved out of the sources of law defining the rights and duties of European nations within a particular context.

Marshall read and worked with the various sources from which the principles of international law were to be gleaned. Henry Wheaton, international legal scholar and Supreme Court reporter during Marshall's tenure on the Court, listed the authoritative sources in his book, *Elements of International Law*, published in 1836:

> 1. Publicists or text writers who defined the approved usage of nations, or the general opinion of the mutual conduct of states as modified by consent during particular periods in history.
> 2. Treaties of peace, alliance and commerce declaring, modifying or defining the international law.
> 3. Various state ordinances prescribing rules for the conduct of commissioned cruisers and prize tribunals.
> 4. Decisions of arbitration boards and prize tribunals.
> 5. The written opinions of officials given to their own governments.
> 6. The history of wars, negotiations, treaties of peace and other transactions relating to the public intercourse of nations.[14]

As the sources indicate, international law "was a body of material in official documents, treatises and textbooks presented as a system of rules purporting to regulate the conduct of states."[15] The sources provided the rules which Marshall adopted and modified to resolve the international issues before him.

Marshall lived in a period subsequently termed the second stage in the evolution of the modern law of nations, a period in which the principles of Emmerich de Vattel (1714-1767), a native of Neuchâtel, were considered paramount.[16] Vattel's influential treatise, which became the authoritative text for the Department of State in the first administrations, was published when Marshall was approximately three years old. When Marshall began practicing law, the literature of international law could be classified into three schools. Initiating the evolutionary process, Hugo Grotius (1583-1645) wrote the first treatise in 1625 which set "forth a general system of law to govern the relations of nations." Grotius, a Dutch scholar, drew upon the ancient Greek and Roman concepts of a "universal society governed by natural law,"[17] and added the concept that societies are also governed by laws to which they consent. Later in the century, the German jurist Samuel Pufendorf (1632-1694) founded the naturalist school, which held that only natural law should control the activities among nations. He specifically denied that consent among nations was a valid source for the law. Writing in the early eighteenth century, a Dutch jurist Cornelius van Bynkershoek (1673-1743) insisted that the primary source for rules governing nations was to be found in consensus among nations. His work which appeared during the thirty-five years before Marshall's birth initiated the positivist school.[18] The literature elaborating these principal schools was extensive. Many treatises on international law were occasioned by specific conflicts and, as such, they were comprehensive legal briefs on particular points of law.[19] The late eighteenth and early nineteenth century legal community in the United States used the treatises to bolster arguments in court and to rationalize various diplomatic positions. Their approach to the sources was ecclectic, and they freely relied on all three schools. Marshall actively participated in this evolutionary phase of international law.

The importance of international law to the United States at this particular period of history cannot be overemphasized.[20] The prevalence and importance of questions whose resolutions depended upon international law dictated that the sources be available. Marshall's participation in public office assured further that he would have access to the materials.[21]

In an informal letter in 1821 congratulating Wheaton on his book, *A Digest of the Law of Maritime Captures and Prizes*, Marshall expressed his deep respect for the law of nations, which he defined as "those moral rules which regulate the communion of man with man."[22] As early as 1793, however, Marshall, in drafting the Virginia Resolutions endorsing Washington's policy of neutrality, signaled the beginning of his study of the law of nations when he maintained that foreign interference in the internal affairs of the United States government constituted a violation of the "laws and usages of nations."[23]

Marshall's dedication to international order and his talent for logical application of law to facts freed him from a parochial background and allowed him to decide international issues legally and objectively. Judicial detachment distinguished his approach from that of his British counterpart, Sir William Scott, Judge of the British High Court of Admiralty. Wheaton recognized that Sir William Scott followed British law on the rights of neutrals when it conflicted with the law of nations.[24] Refusing to follow Scott's precedents on particular points of international law, Marshall observed that although he respected Scott's opinions, he realized that they "lean[ed] strongly in favor of" the British.[25] Marshall considered it essential to have an "upright judiciary which [would] decide impartially between the parties" in international disputes.[26] His decisions reveal that he lived up to that ideal.

Marshall's pre-Court experiences in national government occurred during a time when international events intruded upon domestic affairs to an unusual degree. In this period Marshall first grappled with a host of issues, including confiscation of enemy property (both within the territorial jurisdiction of the United States, as in the debt cases, and on the high seas, as in prize cases), piracy, the rights and duties of neutrals, the law of blockade, the law of contraband, the right of visit, search and seizure, impressment, expatriation, extradition, and the construction of treaty obligations and rights. In formulating decisions on the Court, Marshall drew from the knowledge gained from experience as well as from the various sources for international law. He also relied, of course, on arguments of counsel, as judicial duty required, and applied the persuasive logic of his own mind. From all available sources, Marshall fashioned decisions in public law that gained respect beyond the United States. At the end of the Marshall period, Chancellor Kent noted with satisfaction in his diary, "The English court and Bar are thinking better of us, and study us."[27]

## NOTES

1. Benjamin Munn Ziegler, *The International Law of John Marshall* (Chapel Hill: The University of North Carolina Press, 1939), p. 12, n. 28. For more recent discussions on this aspect of the work of the Supreme Court in the Marshall period, see George Lee Haskins and Herbert A. Johnson, *The Oliver Wendell Holmes Devise History of the Supreme Court of the United States: Foundations of Power: John Marshall, 1801-1815* (New York: Macmillan Publishing Co., 1981) vol. 2, pp. 526-58; and G. Edward White, *The Oliver Wendell Holmes Devise History of the Supreme Court of the United States: The Marshall Court and Cultural Change, 1815-1835* (New York: Macmillan Publishing Co., 1989), vols. 3 and 4, pp. 884-926.

2. William W. Story, ed., "Life, Character, and Services of Chief Justice Marshall: A Discourse pronounced on the 15th of October, 1835, at the request of the Suffolk Bar," *The Miscellaneous Writings of Joseph Story* (Boston: Charles C. Little and James Brown, 1852), pp. 639-97. Justice Story, who knew Marshall well both personally and professionally, remarked on this occasion that Marshall's "attainments in learning . . . were nourished by the solitary vigils of his own genius." *Id.* at p. 646.

3. See also Francis N. Stites, *John Marshall: Defender of the Constitution* (Boston: Little, Brown and Company, 1981), pp. 1-12.

4. Albert J. Beveridge, *The Life of John Marshall: Frontiersman, Soldier, Lawmaker, 1755-1788* (Dunwoody, Ga.: Norman S. Berg, Publisher, 1974), vol. 1, pp. 108-147. Beveridge concluded that "It was his experience, then, on the march, in camp, and on the battlefield that taught John Marshall the primary lesson of the necessity of efficient government." He found that the ability of each state to do "as it pleased" illustrated to Marshall the "absolute need of an efficient central power." *Id.* at 145-47.

5. See generally Beveridge, *The Life of John Marshall*, vol. 1, pp. 69-146, and Leonard Baker, *John Marshall: A Life in Law* (New York: Macmillan Co., Inc., 1974), pp. 26-57.

6. Charles T. Cullen, while associate editor of the Marshall papers, concluded that Marshall spent approximately three months in Williamsburg, "with Wythe reading law and taking notes, attending lectures, arguing in moot court, participating in mock legislatures, and debating with the Phi Beta Kappa Society and other groups." See Charles T. Cullen, "New Light on John Mar-

shall's Legal Education and Admission to the Bar," *The American Journal of Legal History* 16 (1972):345-51 at 348.

7. Marshall appeared at the Fauquier County Court on August 28, 1780, to be sworn as an attorney. Herbert A. Johnson, ed., *The Papers of John Marshall: Correspondence and Papers, November 10, 1775-June 23, 1788, Account Book, September 1783-June 1788* (Chapel Hill: The University of North Carolina Press, 1974), vol. 1, p. 41. n. 9.

8. Marshall served in the House of Delegates from 1782-1785, 1787-1790, and 1795-1796, was a member of the Virginia Executive Council of State (1781-1784), and was Recorder of the Richmond City Hustings Court (1785-1788). See Herbert Alan Johnson, "John Marshall," Leon Friedman and Fred L. Israel, eds., *The Justices of the United States Supreme Court, 1789-1978: Their Lives and Major Opinions* (New York: Chelsea House Publishers, 1980), vol. 1, p. 286.

9. John S. Adams, ed., *An Autobiographical Sketch by John Marshall* (Ann Arbor, Mich.: University of Michigan Press, 1937), p. 17.

10. The speeches were delivered on June 10, June 16 and June 20. See Johnson, ed., *The Papers of John Marshall*, vol. 1., pp. 256-85. Marshall attempted to allay fears against a Federal judiciary in the speech on June 20. He spoke of local concerns and did not allude to the law of nations. He referred to foreign law in illustrating which jurisdiction's law applied to contracts, "If a man contracted a debt in the East-Indies, and it was sued for here, the decision must be consonant to the laws of that country." Contracts were to be determined according to the law of the place where made. Marshall defended this principle, "Is it a novelty?—No—it is a principle in the jurisprudence of this Commonwealth." *Id.*, p. 280. Marshall's response to objections to federal court jurisdiction in controversies between states and foreign states is notable for its brevity:

> Suppose, says he, in such a suit, a foreign State is cast, will she be bound by the decision? If a foreign State brought a suit against the Commonwealth of Virginia, would she not be barred from the claim if the Federal Judiciary thought it unjust? The previous consent of the parties is necessary. And, as the Federal Judiciary will decide, each party will acquiesce. It will be the means of preventing disputes with foreign nations.

*Id.*, p. 281.

11. Alexander DeConde, *A History of American Foreign Policy: Growth to World Power (1700-1914)* (New York: Charles Scribner's Sons, 1978), vol. 1. p. 67.

12. Article I, section 8. Congress is given the power to "define and punish Piracies and Felonies committed on the high seas and Offenses against the Law of Nations." In Article III, the judicial power of the United States is extended "to all Cases, in Law and Equity, arising under this Constitution, the Laws of the United States, and Treaties made, or which shall be made, under their Authority,—to all Cases affecting Ambassadors, other public Ministers

and Consuls;—to all Cases of admiralty and maritime Jurisdiction;—to Controversies to which the United States shall be a Party;—to Controversies. . . between a State, or the Citizens thereof, and foreign States, Citizens or Subjects." In Article VI, Congressional acts made in pursuance of Article I and all Treaties are included with the Constitution as the "supreme Law of the Land." For a discussion of the doctrine of incorporation see Percy E. Corbett, *Law in Diplomacy* (Princeton: Princeton University Press, 1959), pp. 38-42. Attorney General Edmund Randolph in June of 1792 wrote, "The law of nations, although not specifically adopted by the constitution or any municipal act, is essentially a part of the law of the land. Its obligation commences and runs with the existence of a nation, subject to modifications on some points of indifference. . . ." Quoted at p. 39. Blackstone declared that the law of nations was adopted as a part of the common law. See Blackstone, *Commentaries on the Laws of England*, Book 4, ch. 5.

13. James Kent, *Commentaries on American Law* (New York: O. Halsted, 1826), vol. 1, p. 1.

14. Henry Wheaton, *Elements of International Law* (Philadelphia: Lea and Blanchard, 1846, <1836>), vol. 1, i, sec. 15. Wheaton's list is cited because he was a contemporary of Marshall. He was the third Supreme Court reporter succeeding William Cranch in 1815 who had followed the first reporter, Alexander J. Dallas. Wheaton left the job in 1821 to pursue the practice of law, politics, and international diplomacy. A close friend of both John Marshall and William Story, he published two other important works on international law, *A Digest of the Law of Maritime Captures and Prizes* in 1815 and *History of the Law of Nations In Europe and America: From the Earliest Times to the Treaty of Washington, 1842* in English in 1845. The latter was first published in an abbreviated form in French in 1843. See generally Elizabeth Feaster Baker, *Henry Wheaton (1785-1848)* (Philadelphia: University of Pennsylvania Press, 1937). See Charles Pergler, *Judicial Intrepretation of International Law in the United States* (New York: The Macmillan Company, 1928), vol. 1, sec. 6. Pergler stresses that international law is a rule of conduct which has its roots in the needs of civilized states. *Id.* at p. 27. See also Charles Cheney Hyde, *International Law: Chiefly as Interpreted and Applied by the United States* (Boston: Little, Brown, and Company, 1922), vol. 1, sec. 3. Cheney's list basically accords Wheaton's.

15. Percy Elwood Corbett, *The Study of International Law* (New York: Doubleday and Company, Inc., 1955), p. 2. See also Percy Elwood Corbett, *Law and Society in the Relations of States* (New York: Harcourt, Brace and Company, 1959), pp. 17-90.

16. Cornelis van Vollenhoven, *The Three Stages in the Evolution of the Law of Nations* (The Hague: Martinus Nijhoff, 1919), pp. 23-39.

17. Corbett, *The Study of International Law*, pp. 12-15.

18. For a full discussion of the history of international law, see Arthur Nussbaum, *A Concise History of the Law of Nations* (New York: The Macmillan Company, 1954).

19. Grotius wrote *Mare libernum* in 1610 to support the right of the Dutch East India Company to a trade denied by Portugal and Spain. In *Mare clausum*, John Selden defended the right of England in 1635 to dominate portions of the seas. See Corbett, *The Study of International Law*, p. 23.

20. White, *The Marshall Court and Cultural Change*, vols. 3 and 4, pp. 884-926.

21. The availability of the authoritative treatises on international law is reviewed in the 1810 edition of Peter Stephen Du Ponceau's translation of Cornelius Van Bynkershoek, *A Treatise on The Law of War* (Philadelphia: Fry and Kammerer, Printers, 1810), pp. xxiii-xxx. The translator Du Ponceau, a member of the Philadelphia and Supreme Court bars, included an alphabetical list of authorities noting the available translations and dates. The translation is annotated. Both British and United States cases are cited. The translator referred to ten Supreme Court cases and one Massachusetts District Court case. Du Ponceau also indicated when Bynkershoek was wrong, when his opinion did not apply to current matters, and when Du Ponceau disagreed with Bynkershoek's conclusions. Du Ponceau's translation first appeared in *The American Law Journal* founded in 1808 by John E. Hall of the Baltimore bar who filled its pages with topics involving international law. Hall translated for the journal portions of the *Consolato del Mare*, "Of Cases of Recaptures," *The American Law Journal* (Philadelphia: Sergeant Hall, Printer, 1813), vol. 4, p. 299, and published separately a translation of M. Balthazard Marie Emerigon, *An Essay on Maritime Loans* (Baltimore: Philip H. Nicklin & Co., 1811). For the availability of Vattel, see ch. 5, fn. 71. See generally Nussbaum, *A Concise History of the Law of Nations*.

22. John Marshall to Henry Wheaton, March 24, 1821, Wheaton Papers, Als, The Pierpont Morgan Library, New York. MA 995. The terms, *law of nations* and *international law*, are used interchangeably throughout the text of this work.

23. Charles T. Cullen and Herbert A. Johnson, *The Papers of John Marshall: Correspondence and Papers, July 1788-December 1795, Account Book, July 1788-December 1795* (Chapel Hill: The University of North Carolina Press, 1977), vol. 2, p. 197.

24. Henry Wheaton, *A Digest of the Law of Maritime Captures and Prizes* (New York: Forbes & Company, Printers, 1815), p. vi.

25. *The Venus*, 8 Cranch 253, 299 (1814). See also Marshall's instructions to Rufus King, September 20, 1800, when he listed as one of the three complaints against the British, "the unjust decisions of their courts of Vice Admiralty, & the impunity which attends captures totally vexatious & without probable cause of seizure." Charles T. Cullen, ed., *The Papers of John Marshall: Correspondence and Papers, January 1799-October 1800* (Chapel Hill: The University of North Carolina Press, 1984), vol. 4, pp. 288, 294-95. For a thorough review of the contributions made to international law by the highly respected Sir William Scott, see Henry J. Bourguignon, *Sir William Scott, Lord Stowell: Judge of the High Court of Admiralty, 1798-1828*

(New York: Cambridge University Press, 1987).

26. Marshall to King, Charles T. Cullen, *The Papers of John Marshall*, vol. 4, p. 293.

27. William Kent, ed., *Memoirs and Letters of James Kent* (New York: Da Capo Press, 1970 Reprint), p. 267.

# 2

# Attorney and Federalist

On March 2, 1814, Chief Justice John Marshall delivered the opinion of the Court in *Brown v. United States* (1814),[1] a case involving confiscation of enemy property during the War of 1812. Marshall wrote for a less than unanimous Court, as Justice Story's dissent, at least five times longer than Marshall's opinion, was joined by another "of [his] brethren."[2] The case is noteworthy because Marshall broadly discussed the belligerent's right to confiscate enemy property during war, an issue central to the defense in *Ware v. Hylton et al.* (1796),[3] the test case involving pre-Revolutionary war debts and the one case Marshall, as an attorney, argued before the Supreme Court. As Story's dissent indicated, the law of confiscation of enemy property during war was not settled. Marshall's interpretation of the law in the *Brown* case recognized both the "ancient practice of the law of nations" and the law as mitigated "by modern usage in civilized nations."[4] More importantly, Marshall defined the law of nations, expressing an insight gained from his experience in the political branches of the government. He recognized that a rule in the law of nations was, at any given time in history, a product of the political realities of the period: "The rule is addressed to the judgment of the sovereign . . . . [It] is, in its nature, flexible . . . subject to infinite modification . . . not an immutable rule of law, but depends on political considerations which may continually vary."[5]

The case arose out of a dispute over the ownership of cargo of an American-owned ship, the *Emulous*, taken as prize in the War of 1812. London merchants engaged the *Emulous* to deliver cargo to Plymouth, England. The ship sailed from Charlestown, South Carolina, and stopped in Savannah, Georgia, to take on its cargo of 550 tons of timber, 12,000 staves, and 18 tons of lathwood. While in port, it was detained under the April 4, 1812 embargo imposed by Congress on British goods. On April 25, the

*Emulous* was allowed to move to New Bedford, the home of one of the ship's owners, John Delano. The owner had the staves warehoused and the timber floated into a saltwater creek. On November 7, 1812, well after the United States had declared war against England, the London merchants sold the cargo through their agent, Elijah Brown, brother of one of their number, James Brown, to another brother, Armitz Brown. Both the agent and the purchaser were American citizens. When the United States attorney filed the libel suit in the District Court of Massachusetts, he did so on behalf of the United States and the ship's owner, John Delano. The right to libel the ship as war prize was based on the declaration of war against England on June 18, 1812, an event which occurred while the cargo was stored at New Bedford, but still owned by the London merchants. It was four and one-half months after the declaration that the claimant, Armitz Brown, bought the cargo.

Marshall found that the timber could not be condemned as prize of war because a declaration of hostilities did not automatically subject enemy property to confiscation. Legislation specifically authorizing seizure was needed to exercise the right. Marshall reasoned, "The modern rule, then, would seem to be, that tangible property belonging to an enemy and found in the country, at the commencement of war, ought not to be immediately confiscated; and in almost every commercial treaty an article is inserted stipulating the right to withdraw such property."[6]

Marshall considered the modern rule a humane mitigation of the old rule that gave governments an unbridled power of confiscation in time of war. Applying the logic of the debt cases, Marshall concluded, "The universal practice of forebearing to seize and confiscate debts and credits, the principle universally received, that the right to them revives on the restoration of peace, would seem to prove that war is not an absolute confiscation of this property, but simply confers the right of confiscation."[7]

## PRE-COURT EXPERIENCE

Marshall's decision in *Brown* was grounded in the understanding of confiscation that he acquired while serving as co-counsel in the *Ware* case. The dispute over the British debts not only involved legal issues under the law of nations but also concerned government policies with political implications. Marshall participated in both aspects of the dispute. Actively debating the political issues, he became an unofficial spokesman for the administration's foreign policy, which affected the debt collection problems, while in his private capacity, he worked as co-counsel to define the legal issues.

The debt problem presented questions of public law, as comprehended in the Treaty of Peace Between the United States and Great Britain of 1783, in addition to the questions of private law involved in the court cases in which British creditors sought to recover the debts. Laws confiscating or sequestering British debts as enemy property during the Revolution had been passed by several states, including Virginia. At the peace talks in Paris, Britain expressed concern that this legislation would cause collection problems for British creditors, and negotiated to have the issue addressed in the peace treaty. The negotiators agreed that collection of the debts after the war was to be pursued through the courts. Article IV of the peace treaty of 1783 provided that "creditors on either side shall meet with no lawful impediments to the recovery of the full value in sterling money, of all *bona fide* debts heretofore contracted."[8] States, however, continued to treat the debts as enemy property. Under these statutes and in the post-war economic crisis, attempts to collect the debts proved futile.

John Marshall, as attorney (1782-1800), as state legislator (1782-1785, 1787-1790, 1795-1796), as United States representative from Virginia (1799-1800), as Secretary of State (1800-1801), and as Chief Justice of the Supreme Court (1801-1835), participated in both his public and private capacities to resolve the debt problems. From the time he entered public life in 1782 as a member of the Virginia House of Delegates, when the Treaty of Paris was being negotiated, Marshall became a participant in various activities relating to the British debts. As Chief Justice in the *Brown* case, he announced the opinion incorporating the law that, he had earlier been instrumental in developing.[9]

To understand Marshall's contribution, it will be necessary to examine the emergence of the debt issue as a political cause, to explore Marshall's public performance in the state and national legislatures and the cabinet, and to scrutinize his defense arguments for debtors in private actions by British creditors. The impact of the Revolution on prewar debts owed to British subjects was direct and immediate and rendered the private law inadequate to deal with the issue, which became primarily one of policy.[10] Marshall's experiences demonstrate the divergent attempts to solve the problem and reveal that a knowledge of international law concepts was necessary to address the issues fully.

## The Debt Issue as a Political Cause

Following the Treaty of Paris, political hostility to Great Britain continued unabated, exacerbating the problems that British creditors encountered when they attempted to collect the debts. Increasing domestic tensions further complicated the issue during the first years of Washington's administration, as the Hamiltonian and Jeffersonian factions formulated their differences over domestic as well as foreign issues. When France and England declared war in 1793, the emerging political parties, already distinquished by pro-British and pro-French sentiments, deepened their respective foreign loyalties. The new French Minister, Citizen Edmond C. Genêt, after arriving in the United States on April 8, 1793, openly courted American support for the French. President

Washington responded on April 22, 1793, with the Proclamation of Neutrality.

Marshall, for the first time, publicly embraced the administration's policy. In the political debate that followed the proclamation, as "Aristides" and "Gracchus," he answered James Monroe's "Agricola" pro-French arguments, and discussed fully the British debt issue.[11] The newspaper debate was occasioned when Marshall, reacting to the criticism of the proclamation, organized a public meeting in Richmond on August 17. George Wythe served as president of the meeting, which endorsed the administration's policy of strict neutrality and denounced Genêt.[12] The Republicans responded by conducting pro-French meetings and by taking the fight to the newspapers.[13] Carefully avoiding criticizing the president, the Republicans called for united support for the French cause. They denounced their opponents as pro-British and invoked long-standing complaints that the British had not fulfilled their treaty obligations to vacate the western forts and to compensate masters for slaves taken away during the Revolution. The British, however, justified their non-compliance by the fact that the pre-Revolutionary War debts owed British subjects had not been paid. Marshall analyzed these complaints in the essays prompted by the Genêt affair. Marshall's political reputation, which until this time had been confined to being, on the state level, a "creditor-minded nationalist"[14] and a friend of "energetic government and fiscal orthodoxy,"[15] took on a national dimension.

During these political debates, Marshall not only announced the political orientation that he would hold throughout his Chief Justiceship, but he also expressed a basic understanding of the principle attribute of a sovereign nation in a world of nations. He did so in the first essay when he characterized the resolutions adopted by the Richmond Federalist meeting in August. The resolutions, he noted, approved "the conduct of the President of the United States towards the belligerent powers of Europe" and expressed "detestation and abhorrence of any interference whatever of a foreign nation or minister with [the United States'] political contests or internal government."[16]

Marshall saw in the rising Republican opposition both a repudiation of national union and a tendency erroneously to equate national interest with French or foreign interest. He had taken the cause of the Federalists in the Virginia Ratification Convention in 1788 and argued for a strong national government. In domestic affairs, he opted for national sovereignty over state autonomy. Now, in an international context, he was asserting his belief in the sovereignty of the United States, free from the control of other sovereign nations. In Virginia, however, where the ideology of Republicanism with its emphasis on states' rights was rapidly gaining control, Marshall was in the minority.

As "Gracchus," Marshall revealed a thorough understanding of the politics of the British debt issue. Monroe as "Agricola" faulted the administration for failing to require the British to honor their treaty obligations of 1783. He rejected the British argument that legal impediments prevented debt collection by insisting that the United States had fulfilled its duty under the peace treaty by including the clause providing that no impediments would be made to the collection of British debts and thereafter adopting the Constitution making treaty obligations superior to offending state laws. Monroe stressed that the British had not complied with the treaty and demanded that the administration insist on compliance. Marshall answered the argument by reviewing the history of British attempts to collect the debts through the courts:

> As Agricola rests his censure on the government, upon the perfect execution of the treaty on our part, it cannot be improper to examine the truth of his assertion. In the year 1789, the foederal courts were constituted, and many suits for British debts were immediately instituted. Whether they were recoverable or not, is known to have been a question of serious doubt, and pleas in bar of the action were generally filed. Until the last term, no opinion of the court was given, and it is a known fact that to this moment not a single judgment has been rendered, where a plea has been filed.

He then struck at the heart of Monroe's argument.

> [I]t is not readily to be admitted, that the adoption of the constitution executed the treaty, while judgments were denied, nor could it truly have been stated by our executive, that there was no bar to the recovery of British debts, while that very question was undecided, and seriously agitating in our courts.[17]

Marshall insisted that the negotiations concerning treaty compliance were ongoing and that Great Britain had a legitimate argument against the United States:

> We cannot say that the government of the United States has not received assurances, that the western posts will be delivered to us, so soon as British debts shall be adjudged recoverable. On the contrary, we have reason to suppose, that some such assurances have been received— . . . there is reason to suppose, the executive has received some assurances that the posts will be delivered up, when every impediment to the recovery of British debts shall be removed. . . . It is admitted that Britain has never claimed a right to the western posts, but has ever avowed that she held them only as pledges, to secure a compliance with the treaty on the part of America.[18]

Concluding the political argument, Marshall admitted that he was "by no means satisfied with the conduct of the British," and that he resented "the ill disposition manifested by that nation towards" the United States. However, he could find "no cause for transferring that resentment to our own government."[19]

In his biography of George Washington published in 1804-1805, Marshall described the international political climate surrounding the events of 1793. The description was consistent with the political analysis he expressed as "Gracchus." "The proclamation of neutrality which was treated as a royal edict, was not only considered as assuming powers not belonging to the executive, and, as evidencing the monarchical tendencies of that department, but as demonstrating the disposition of the government to break its connections with France, and to dissolve the friendship which united the people of the two republics."[20]

Marshall explained that the Jeffersonians, as an "active and powerful party openly and decidedly embraced the principles" of Mr. Genêt and with "infectious enthusiasm . . . contended that there was a natural and inveterate hostility between monarchies and republics," insisting that the administration's "combination against France was a combination against liberty in every part of the world; and that the destinies of America were inseparably linked with those of the French republic."[21]

Marshall maintained the political beliefs developed during the 1790 debates throughout his life and continued to think that Republican opposition to the administrations of Washington and Adams, motivated primarily by pro-French feelings, was inimical to the survival of the United States as a nation. Although the intensity of his own feelings about foreign influence remained intact, the United States firmly established its national identity and the pro-French and pro-British sentiments of the 1790's gradually abated. Marshall, however, never ceased to criticize and express apprehension about Republican policies. In 1832, he complained to Justice Story that Republicans theories were "incompatable with a government for more than a single state. We can form no union which shall be closer than an alliance among sovereigns. . . . We are now gathering the bitter fruits of the tree . . . planted by Mr. Jefferson, and so industriously and perseveringly cultivated by Virginia."[22]

When President Andrew Jackson issued the Nullification Proclamation, Marshall's Washingtonian Federalism remained intact:

> Imitating the Quaker who said that the dog he wished to destroy was mad, they said Andrew Jackson had become a Federalist, even an ultra Federalist. To have said that he was ready to break down and trample on every other department of the government would not have injured him, but to say he was a Federalist—a convert to the opinions of Washington, was a mortal blow under which he is yet staggering.[23]

Although committed as well to the domestic policies of the Federalists, Marshall's political contribution related to foreign policy. He was motivated to justify foreign policy in an area that required an understanding of international law.

## Marshall's Contribution in Public Office

As a state legislator in Virginia first elected to office in 1782, Marshall became fully aware of the controversy surrounding the Virginia Sequestration Act of 1777. During the Revolution, the Virginia House of Delegates passed the act authorizing payment into the state treasury of all debts owed to the enemy.[24] Debtors who paid into the treasury, of course, assumed that they had thus satisfied their obligations. The Virginia act was typical of those passed by the various state legislatures during the Revolution.

Aware that these acts posed a threat to collection by British merchants, the British ministers in Paris attempted during the peace negotiations to secure the British creditors' rights to collect their debts. Richard Oswald, the British negotiator, reported from Paris to Secretary of State Thomas Townshend on October 2, 1782, that he had discussed the problem of debt confiscations with John Jay, who with Benjamin Franklin, John Adams, and Henry Laurens represented the Americans at the conference table. "Mr. Jay replied that he had heard of no such confiscations but in the province of Maryland, which he seemed not to approve of."[25]

Approximately one month after Oswald indicated his belief that the Commissioners could do nothing about the confiscations and that he would not press the issue, Henry Strachey, Undersecretary of State, submitted the treaty terms to Townshend noting, "The Recovery of the Property of the Refugees, and of the Debts due to British Subjects before and since the War, are points which have been obstinately fought for. You will see by the Treaty all that could be obtained. The Debts prior to 1775 appear to be safe. Those since that period were alleged to have been illegal and therefore not recoverable but under the Honor of those who contracted them."[26]

The British Commissioners insisted that "honest debts must be honestly paid in honest money."[27] The American Commissioners acquiesced in the British view. Strachey, discussing the treaty terms with the negotiators on November 25, 1782 stressed the agreement on debt collection, "The Point regarding the Debts, though somewhat altered in the Forms of Expression, is exactly as you put it, in respect to substance."[28]

On December 13, the four American Commissioners reported to secretary for foreign affairs under the Confederation government, Robert R. Livingston. They considered Article IV on the debt issue "founded in Justice and good Policy" and expressed the opinion that "no acts of government could dissolve the Obligations of good Faith resulting from lawfull Contracts, between Individuals of the two Countries, prior to the War."[29] Livingston agreed that "No honest Man could wish to withhold [payment]," but he cautioned that "[a] little forebearance in British creditors till people have recovered in part from the losses sustained by the war will be necessary to render the Article palatable, and indeed to secure more effectually the debt."[30]

Realizing that economic problems would be experienced in the aftermath of the Revolution and that hardship would result from immediately enforcing the debt obligations, Livingston instructed the peace ministers to negotiate for time. The ministers in July of 1783 responded to Livingston's concern. "We shall immediately propose an Article to be inserted in the Definitive Treaty for Postponing the Payment of British Debts for the Time mentioned by Congress."[31] A three-year delay was suggested, but the provision was never incorporated. Article IV of the peace treaty finalized on September 3, 1783, merely provided that creditors would not be legally impeded from seeking their remedies. The British were obligated under Article VII to return the slaves detained and carried away by them during the war. As late as May 28, 1783, Livingston, anticipating yet another compliance problem, advised the Americans negotiators that the British were violating the 7th article of the treaty by "sending off the slaves under pretence that the proclamations has set them free, as if a British general had, either by their laws or those of nations, a right of proclamation to deprive any man of his property."[32]

The following June, the Virginia House of Delegates, John Marshall among them, entertained several items of business concerning the British debts. On June 7, 1784, the House appointed a committee to inquire into the "infraction on the part of Great Britain, of the seventh article of peace between the [two countries], so far as the same respects the detention of slaves and other property, belonging to the citizens of the Commonwealth."[33] A committee of five, which included Patrick Henry was appointed.[34] On the same day that the House of Delegates appointed the committee to investigate British non-compliance, the following resolution was voted down (57 to 37): "Resolved, That so much of all and every act or acts of Assembly, now in force in this Commonwealth, as prevents a due compliance with the stipulations contained in the definitive treaty entered into between Great Britain and America ought to be repealed."[35] The resolution, if passed, would have placed the Virginia legislators firmly on the side of enforcing the debt obligations of Virginians as required by the treaty. Marshall voted with the minority in favor of the resolution.

The committee investigating British noncompliance proposed resolutions in their report of June 14, which the House debated on June 22 and 23. The House instructed their representatives in Congress to ask that a remonstrance be sent to England requesting payment for unreturned slaves. They were further instructed to use the payment of debts as a bargaining chip. Virginia would "refuse to comply with article 4, providing for debt recovery, if reparations were not paid." When the reparations were paid, "the General Assembly would repeal all laws inhibiting the recovery" of the debts and arrange for their repayment.[36] Later the same year, Marshall referred to these resolutions and expressed his personal sentiments, indicating the reasons for his conclusions, in a letter to James Monroe. "I wish with you that our

Assembly had never passed those resolutions respecting the British debts which have been so much the subject of reprehension throughout the States. I wish it because it affords a pretext to the British to retain possession of the forts on the lakes but much more because I ever consider it as a measure tending to weaken the federal bonds which in my conception are too weak already."[37]

Counsel for a British creditor seeking to recover in 1804 a pre-Revolutionary War debt summarized the various legal impediments imposed by Virginia during this period. He argued that he was prevented by the laws from bringing his claim within the time prescribed by law.[38]

> The first impediment was caused by the expiration of the fee bill on the 12th of December, 1774, whereby the courts of justice were shut against all persons. This impediment was general, and continued until the commencement of the war, on the 19th of April, 1775.
> From this period until the peace, in September, 1783, the state of war prevented British subjects from bringing suits in our courts, if no other impediments had existed. The first act of the assembly of Virginia, . . . is that passed in October, 1777, sequestering British property and suspending executions, . . . The 2d act of impediment is that of November, 1781 . . . to suspend execution in certain cases. The 3d is the act of May, 1782 . . . to repeal so much of a former act as suspends the issuing executions upon certain judgments until December, 1783. The 4th is the act of October, 1782, to amend [the preceding act]. . . . The 5th is the act of December, 1783, . . . to revive and continue in force the several acts of the assembly for suspending the issuing of executions on certain judgments until December, 1783. . . . This last act expired in July, 1784.
> . . . But these impediments did not cease at that period, but were still continued by the acts of 1785 and 1787. In addition . . . were the decisions of juries and courts of law who supported the plea in bar that the plaintiff was a British subject.[39]

Resistance to the enforcement of British debt obligations was intense. Under the peace treaty, creditor recourse to the courts was the method of recovery. State courts and juries, however, were reluctant to enforce the contracts. When the federal court system was put into place by the Judiciary Act of 1789, another forum for enforcement was technically available. The forum was open, but recovery was not forthcoming.[40] Creditors met the same resistance in federal courts that they met in the state courts. Not until 1796, when the Supreme Court delivered its opinion in the *Ware v. Hylton et al.* test case, did the British creditor have a confirmed right to recover. The court ruled that the treaty prohibition against impediments to collection was superior to state laws impinging upon the right to collect.

The facts in the test case indicate the overriding public dimensions inherent in the dispute. In the initial filing, William Jones, surviving partner of a British firm, Farrel and Jones, sued to collect on a bond against Daniel Hylton and Company and Francis Eppes. The bond for 2,976 pounds, 11 shillings, and 6d. sterling was dated July 4, 1774. On December 20, 1777, the Virginia legislature passed the sequestration act providing that:

> it may and shall be lawful for any citizen of this commonwealth owing money to a subject of Great Britain to pay the same, or any part thereof, from time to time, as he shall think fit, into the said loan office, taking thereout a certificate for the same; in the name of the creditor, with an endorsement under the hand of the commissioner of the said office, expressing the name of the payer, and shall deliver such certificate to the governor and counsel, whose receipt shall discharge him from so much of the said debt.[41]

Relying on the sequestration act, Hylton, a Richmond merchant, paid the full amount of the indebtedness into the loan office on April 26, 1780. The governor, Thomas Jefferson, signed Hylton's receipt on May 30, 1780.[42] The holding in the test case, *Ware v. Hylton et al.*, confirmed the private right to collect, but it was in reality a hollow victory. The exercise of this private contractual right "secured" by the treaty worked havoc on debtors like Hylton who had suffered tremendous losses during the war.[43] Hylton's post-trial fate illustrated not only the problems debtors encountered as a result of adverse judgments but also the problems creditors faced after receiving a favorable judgment when attempting to use the full planopy of remedies available to them. When Hylton lost the case, the jury assessed damages against him for $5,418.00 in addition to $596.00 plus interest.[44] To satisfy the judgment, execution was "levied on 36 slaves, five horses, two mules, thirty head of cattle, twenty-four head of sheep, and three hundred barrels of Indian corn." Hylton posted bond but subsequently defaulted. The creditor was forced to levy on the property. His property exhausted by legal process, Hylton was forced into debtor's prison. From his release in 1801 until his death in 1811, he lived as a salaried clerk.[45]

John Marshall, in his defense for Hylton, addressing the injustice of double payment, argued that the debt had been paid by Hylton to the state, that the state should be considered the debtor under the circumstances, and that the words of the treaty were not sufficiently plain in describing the term "debtors." Marshall argued that "[t]he words ought surely, to be very plain, that shall work so evident a hardship, as to compel a man to pay a debt, which he had before extinquished."[46] This argument would have kept the solution in the public arena—the state of Virginia, as debtor, would pay. Because Hylton had paid into the state treasury, the right to collect the debt against the private citizen was extinquished. The creditor should be paid by the state. Jefferson, who was governor of Virginia in 1778-1780, also believed that the state was holding the funds for the British creditors. He explained how the act should work:

> Every one is sensible how this is to be ultimately settled. Neither the British creditor, nor the state will be permitted to lose by these paiments. The debtor will be credited with what he paid according to what it was really worth at the time he paid it, and he must pay the balance. Nor does he lose by this: for if a man, who owed 1000 dollars to a British merchant, paid 800 paper dollars into the treasury when the depreciation was at 8 for 1, it is clear he paid but 100 real dollars, & must now pay 900.[47]

While the arguments were being advanced before the Circuit Court in Virginia and in the Supreme Court in the *Ware* case, negotiations were being pursued by the United States and Britain to reach an agreement over the debt issue. These negotiations culminated in the Jay Treaty of 1794.[48] Under Article VI, a Commission of five was set up to determine compensation in those cases where adequate recovery was prevented by law. The United States agreed to make "full and complete compensation" in such cases. The Commission's jurisdiction was limited to creditors' claims that could not be collected because of "lawful impediments." The Commission was not empowered to settle claims unrecoverable because of debtor insolvency or creditor "delay," "negligence," or "wilful omission" in prosecuting.[49] The Article thus considered those debts rendered uncollectable by state action to be public debts recoverable from the federal government. Arguments in the *Ware* test case began on February 9, 1796. The treaty was proclaimed on February 29, and judgment was rendered in *Ware* a week later on March 7. In slightly more than one week, the court had reaffirmed the right to collect debts in the courts and the negotiators had provided that those which were uncollectable through the courts would be paid by the national government. The issue appeared to be solved.

The arbitration commission set up in the Jay Treaty was composed of two British and two United States Commissioners. The fifth Commissioner, chosen by lot, was also British. When faced with the task of appointing the two American Commissioners, President Washington inquired of the Attorney General of Virginia, Charles Lee, whether Marshall would accept appointment. Lee assured Washington that Marshall would not serve, although he was qualified and he was not a debtor under the terms of the Article.[50]

The Commission met in Philadelphia in 1797 and heard claims for two years. They were unable to formulate workable principles. The British insisted that any debt "fairly contracted before the peace" that remained unpaid in whole or in part "in sterling money . . . at the peace" came within the jurisdiction of the Commission.[51] They also wished to include interest during the war and to hear Loyalist claims. The United States Commissioners disagreed and withdrew. No further meetings were held after July 1799.[52]

John Marshall addressed the breakdown of negotiations in the House of Representatives and as Secretary of State. When he was a member of the House, the arbitration commission had disbanded. In the House response to President Adams's December 1799 speech to the representatives, Marshall regretted the breakdown of the debt negotiations and noted that the House "would not adopt a construction of the Article" that would allow Great Britain to extend the Commission's jurisdiction "beyond [that created by] the instrument."[53] Marshall further expressed the hope that the British would "disclaim such extension" and "bring the business committed to" the Commission to a conclusion.[54]

When Marshall became Secretary of State in June of 1800, he again had the occasion to defend the acts of the United States Commissioners on the grounds that the British Commissioners had tried to extend their lawful jurisdiction.[55] In the State Department, Marshall's observations were addressed fully to Rufus King, the United States Minister in London. King was under instructions from the former Secretary of State Timothy Pickering to arrange diplomatic discussions to present "explanatory articles" that would provide rules for future commission meetings. King wrote to Pickering on April 22, 1800, but the report was not received until July 23, 1800 after Marshall became Secretary. King revealed that the British foreign secretary, Lord William Grenville, had made overtures for the "Settlement of the Claims of the British creditors by the payment of a gross sum to their government."[56] Marshall advised President Adams that "Under these circumstances, it woud I think be the real interest of the United States to pay, perhaps more than we believe to be really due, rather than risk the arbitration."[57]

During the month of August, Marshall consulted with Adams and other members of the cabinet to determine the "sum in gross" that would be the "ultimatum" the United States would agree to offer. Adams preferred to use explanatory articles to settle the issue. His second choice would be a sum in gross, hopefully less than "a million sterling."[58] He felt that the difficulty of arriving at an agreeable sum would "be the greatest" problem, and he disregarded Marshall's concern that the French might be affronted by the negotiations by insisting, "We surely have a right to pay our honest debts in the manner least inconvenient to ourselves."[59] Responding to Adam's suggestion to consult with the cabinet, Marshall reported that their consensus was to "give 5 million of dollars in satisfaction of all claims under the 6th Article."[60] Marshall explained specifically that such a sum in gross would not cover all prewar debts:

> The claims of the British creditors woud not by such a compact be extinguishd as against American debtors. Our courts woud still be open to them & their rights woud be the same as heretofore: but their claim against the American nation for those

> debts which had been lost or diminishd by impediments created by the diffirent states woud be extinguishd by the new compact & the receipt on the part of their government of the stipulated satisfaction for such claims.[61]

Adams communicated his understanding of the issue to Marshall on August 26 when he wrote, "five millions of Dollars are more than sufficient, provided The British Creditors are left at Liberty to prosecute in our Courts and recover all the Debts which are now recoverable."[62] And on August 30, he reiterated his preference for explanatory articles.[63]

On August 23, Marshall wrote to King summarizing the cabinet's thinking on Article VI. He instructed King to "renew application to Lord Grenville" that explanatory articles be adopted to assure that a properly instructed commission would act within jurisdictional limits.[64] King should, if the explanatory articles proved unattainable, offer a "gross sum in full compensation of all claims made or to be made on the United States government under Article 6, the amount of 4 m. dollars would be deemed satisfactory—but in no event should the sum exceed One million sterling."[65]

In a separate letter, marked "Private," written on the same day, Marshall indicated to King that those in the administration most knowledgeable in the claims of British creditors believed "on a fair & honorable construction" of Article VI, British claims "woud not exceed two milion, or at most two & a half milion of dollars."[66]

The dispute was not settled while Marshall was Secretary of State. Under the Jefferson administration, the Convention of January 8, 1802 concluded the matter. The Convention annulled Article VI of the Jay Treaty of 1794 and reaffirmed Article IV of the Treaty of Paris of 1783. Between 1803 and 1811, the United States paid in three installments the lump sum of 600,000 pounds sterling ($2,664,000.) to satisfy British claims rendered uncollectable by legal impediments. Private rights of creditors with collectable debts continued to be pursued through the courts. The public liability of the United States was discharged.[67]

Albert J. Beveridge contends that "King settled the controversy according to the instructions of Marshall. But the Republicans, being then in power, claimed the credit."[68] Beveridge considers it "one of the curious turns of history that Marshall, as Secretary of State, made the proposition that finally concluded the matter and that Jefferson consummated the transaction."[69] The suggestion, however, that a lump sum be offered to settle the debt disputes came from Lord Grenville, as Beveridge acknowledges.[70]

While participating in the government's attempts to solve the debt dispute, Marshall was aware of public resentment of debt collection. It is apparent from the private letter that accompanied the instructions to Rufus King on August 23, 1800, that Marshall, as a matter of public policy, preferred to settle the individual debts by arbitration with a properly instructed commission exercising a limited jurisdiction. In the letter, he expressed the opinion that the "[irritation] of the public mind" against Great Britain would be increased and that a lump sum payment would be considered" a disgraceful sacrafice with wh[ich] the Govt have purchased the continuance of a humiliating peace." But he added that "[t]hese considerations will not & ought not to induce the government of the United States to decline a measure of public utility."[71] Marshall's sense of the public good prevailed and he appeared to have lost his reservations about the risks of arbitration.

### Legal Arguments in the *Ware* Case

Marshall necessarily studied the legal principles involved in the debt dispute while representing numerous Virginia debtors. The pre-revolutionary debts were concentrated in Virginia where it "was estimated there were more than $2,000,000 of such British debts."[72] British creditors in February of 1791 estimated the total debt to be £4,930,656, 13 shillings, 1 pence with Virginia's portion almost one-half (3/7), at £2,305,408, 19 shillings, 1 pence.[73] Virginia's sequestration act of 1777 "was shown by cases before the commissioners in Philadelphia" to be "one of the most mischievous in obstructing the execution of the fourth article of the peace treaty."[74] In addition to other acts, Virginia had passed a law in 1782 that prevented recovery of a British debt assigned to a Virginia citizen unless the assignment had been made prior to 1777.[75] Creditors were therefore prevented from approaching the courts through agents. British creditors, anticipating better treatment in the federal courts, began to pursue their claims there after 1789. John Marshall was retained during the 1790's by Virginia defendants in over 100 debt cases.[76] He undertook the defense of some twenty debtors who had made payments into the state loan office, with the primary argument being that the debt had been paid.

Defense counsel against the British creditors developed elaborate pleas to deny liability. After generally denying the debt by pleading payment or *nil debit* (do not owe), counsel entered special pleas. All of these pleas were used in the test case, *Jones v. Walker* (1790-97),[77] which through death and substitution of parties on appeal became *Ware v. Hylton et al.* (1796). The Supreme Court in the *Ware* case ruled against the debtor on all counts. The debt pleas were predicated on the rights and duties of nations at war. Marshall used them in his defense of Dr. Thomas Walker and Daniel Hylton.

1. Pleading specially, Marshall noted that payment of the debt had been made pursuant to the sequestration act of 1777 and claimed satisfaction and discharge "from so much of the debt" specified as paid in the appended or recited loan office certificate.[78]

2. The debtor then relied upon discharge of the debt by virtue of a Virginia act passed in 1779 that provided that real and personal property belonging to British subjects within Virginia vested in the commonwealth by virtue of escheat and forfeiture. The act specifically mentioned "land slaves and other

real estate" but the debtor argued that debts were personal property also covered by the act.[79]

3. Counsel pleaded exoneration of the debt by British noncompliance with treaty obligations and further acts of hostility. The printed plea alleged that his "Majesty hath wilfully broken & violated the sd treaty in this that his Britannic Majesty hath from the day of said treaty & ever since continued to carry of[f] the negroes . . . & still doth refuse to deliver them or permit the owners of said negroes to take them . . . and . . . hath & still doth refuse to withdraw his armies and garrisons from every port place & harbor of the United States." In addition to not yielding up the territory as required, the British were accused by the debtor of supplying "arms ammunition & weapons of war, to wit . . . guns gun powder, lead, leaden bulletts, Tomahawks & scalping knives" to the Indians warring with the United States and of purchasing from the Indians plunder taken from United States citizens.[80]

4. In the last plea, counsel alleged that the debt had been annulled. Having been contracted by and between two British subjects before July 4, 1776, the date the government under which it was contracted was dissolved, the debt had no legal validity.[81]

Marshall's arguments in the test case reveal that he had studied the publicists of international law and had used these authorities to substantiate the allegations in the pleas. Two sources survive to elucidate his reasoning for the debtor's defense: (1) recently published notes of Marshall's argument taken by Supreme Court Justice James Iredell when he sat in the Circuit Court trial on May 29 and 30, 1793,[82] and (2) notes taken by Marshall's opposing counsel, William Tilghman, which were used by the court reporter, Alexander J. Dallas, in his published report of the case argued before the Supreme Court on February 9, 1796. Dallas was not present during the arguments and a comparison of the Tilghman notes with the published report indicates that Dallas relied almost completely on the Tilghman notes.[83]

Iredell's notes reveal extensive reference to the international law publicists. Marshall cited Emmerich de Vattel's *The Law of Nations, or the Principles of Natural Law Applied to the Conduct and the Affairs of Nations and of Sovereigns* at least six times, referring to the introduction and to Books 2 and 3. He cited two chapters in Book 3 of Hugo Grotius's *The Rights of War and Peace*; two volumes of J. J. Burlamaqui's *The Principles of Natural and Political Law*; and Book 8 of Samuel Pufendorf's *On the Law of Nature and Nations*. Iredell's notes also contain a reference to Cornelius van Bynkershoek's *A Treatise on the Law of War*, which indicates that Marshall left this authority to be argued later by his co-counsel, James Innes.

The official report and the Tilghman notes from which it was taken indicates that Marshall cited only Vattel.[84]

This evidence refutes the traditional opinion of Marshall's scholarship. As his institutional education consisted of only a few months of attendance in 1780 at lectures given by George Wythe at The College of William and Mary, it has been generally reported that he depended upon counsel to enlighten him about issues that came before him on the Supreme Court. The references to many treatises with notations not only to the authority but also to page, number and section suggest that Marshall's informal schooling in law during his sixteen years of private practice was an adequate substitute for formal training. Opinions such as those expressed by political scientist and biographer Benjamin Munn Ziegler must be revised to reflect the newer understanding of Marshall's studies. Ziegler contended that Marshall's "legal training was notably weak, and in the field of international law was conspicuous only by its absence."[85] Ziegler concluded that Marshall acquired some knowledge of international law from negotiating with France as special envoy, but he emphasized that Marshall was able to "create and embody in a masterly series of opinions that distinctively American conception of international law" by instructive briefs from the brilliant international lawyers who practiced in the Supreme Court.[86]

As late as 1955, legal scholar Edward Dumbauld in a law review article stated, "Much of Marshall's learning in the realm of international law was derived from Thomas Rutherford's *Institutes of Natural Law*. This digest of Grotius was one of the few law books in Marshall's library. It was an influential treatise in that era, and Marshall relied extensively on its teachings."[87]

However, in the British debt cases, Marshall, who was noted for his diligence, mastered his subject, *inter alia*, by direct recourse to learned international law treatises. The available evidence indicates that Marshall was well schooled in international law through his pre-Court study and experiences at a time when legal education was not a formal study. This interpretation is consistent with the state of legal education available in the United States during this period.[88]

Co-counsel arguments at the initial hearing of the test case relied extensively on the principles of international law. *Jones v. Walker*, the original test case was first heard on November 24, 1791, before Associate Supreme Court Justices Thomas Johnson and John Blair and District Judge Cyrus Griffin. Marshall associated with Patrick Henry, Alexander Campbell, and James Innes as co-counsel for Walker's defense. William Wirt's *Sketches of the Life and Character of Patrick Henry* contains the only report of the trial arguments. As Henry was co-counsel with Marshall, these arguments are instructive of the understanding and strategy shared by the attorneys in the case. They are also consistent with the arguments by Marshall for which we have records at the Circuit and Supreme Court level. Wirt, who practiced often before the Supreme Court as a private attorney and as Attorney General, reported that Henry "came forth, on this occasion, a perfect master of every principle of law, national and municipal, which touched the subject of investigation in the most distant point."[89] The substantive portions of Henry's speech illustrated the range of counsel's learning and understanding of international law in this area. Marshall's arguments in 1793 at the Circuit Court level and in 1796 at the Supreme Court level continued his reliance on these international law concepts, on which the defense pleas were originally predicated.

Henry's speech was a discourse on the meaning of international law. Henry "cite[d] and read[] copious extracts from Grotius and Vattel" to support his contentions that enemy debts are subject to forfeiture and confiscation in both "common" and revolutionary wars, that all enemy property, both corporeal and incorporeal (the latter would include enemy debts) were included, and that all nations were equal with "powers as extensive and unlimited as any other nation."[90] Henry's arguments claimed the rights of nations described by the text-writers for the United States, "Those authors state, in language as emphatic and nervous as the human mind can conceive, or the human tongue can utter, that independent nations have the power of confiscating the property of their enemies; and so this gallant nation . . . America, being a sovereign and complete nation . . . possessed all the rights of the most powerful and ancient nations.[91] He used the same sources to bolster his contention that in a civil war, the parties "are to be considered as two distinct peoples . . . and to govern themselves in the conduct of the war by the general law of nations."[92]

Henry attempted to answer opposing counsel's reliance on Vattel for the proposition that debts were an exception to the general rule of confiscation. He repeated the citation to Vattel and attempted to show that it did not apply to the British debts, as the exception to confiscation was based on consent. "But at present, in regard to the advantage and safety of commerce, all the sovereigns of Europe have departed from this rigour." Henry explained, "The author says, that although a nation has a right to confiscate debts due by its people to an enemy, yet *at present the custom of Europe is contrary.*"[93] Henry argued that although the exception existed in Europe, it could not apply in the United States because "to make this customary law obligatory, the assent of all the parties to be bound by it is necessary."[94] The United States was not bound because it had not agreed to the exception. Quoting Vattel, he supported the necessity for consent:

> These three kinds of the law of nations, *voluntary, conventional* and *customary*, together, compose the *positive law of nations*. For they all proceed from the volition of nations; the *voluntary law*, from their presumed consent: the *conventional law*, from an express consent; and the *customary law , from a tacit consent*: and as there can be no other manner of deducing any law from the will of nations, there are only these three kinds of the *positive law of nations*.[95]

Henry quoted Vattel, book and page, to prove, "by the same great writer," that when war is declared against an unjust enemy, a "nation has a right of doing against the enemy whatever is necessary to th[e] justiciable end of bringing him to reason, and obtaining justice and security."[96] Henry reasoned that Virginia was forced by the "want of an exchequer" not only to confiscate the debts, but also to "emit paper money, and compel our citizens to receive it for gold."[97] Necessity provided the basis for requiring debts to be paid in currency.

These portions of Henry's speech reveal in detail the strategy used by the defense. Referring extensively to the rules and principles of international law, counsel's tactic "was to turn a private dispute into a public controversy between Great Britain and America."[98] This strategy continued to be used during the long circuitous path the test case took through the courts.

There was no decision on the merits of the case after this first hearing, which lasted over a week. The case came up again in May 1793 under the style of *Ware v. Hylton et al.*. William Jones, the original plaintiff, had died, and John Tyndale Ware was appointed his executor. Counsel for the defendant, Dr. Walker, had not made the necessary filings to be on the docket. The claim against Walker was continued, and the parties agreed to pursue plaintiff's claims against Hylton, whose defense was identical to Walker's. Hylton hired Marshall, Patrick Henry and Alexander Campbell in April of 1793 to join his already retained counsel, James Innes. The issues, arguments, and counsel were thus in place for the second hearing in the test case.

Marshall's arguments at the second hearing can be roughly approximated by using Iredell's notes. He contended that the sequestration act of 1777 formed a bar to recovery of the debts and that Virginia's legislative acts had the full weight and authority of an individidual nation because "[a]t that time the Government could only legislate *by means of State Legislatures*."[99]

He cited Grotius and Vattel for the laws of war that condoned confiscation of enemy property, reasoned that debts, although personal and intangible, were subject to confiscation as well as property, visible and tangible. Like Henry, Marshall argued that the general rule allowing confiscation of debts applied, the "particular exception [thereto] not allowable."[100] He argued further that the "Act of 1777 makes Gov. a Debtor," thus continuing the strategy of placing the debts within the public responsibility. The debtor was discharged, Marshall contended, of "so much of the debt" as the receipt indicated he had paid to the state.[101]

Iredell's notes also suggest how Marshall reconciled the treaty requirement that no legal impediments thwart recovery with the debtor's reliance on a law absolving him of responsibility. Iredell noted, "Treaty the law of the Land, & Judges bound to take notice. A refusal to render Judgment for P. no cause of War to G.B. Deny only a present right of the P. Vattel 2 Book s. 257. Whole Treaty must be looked into—If broke not sanctioned."[102] The notes indicate explicitly that Marshall accepted the treaty as binding, and that he meticulously fashioned his argument to recognize and avoid the effect of the treaty. The argument supported the defense that the debtor was absolved of his duty because Great Britain had also violated the treaty terms. The notes suggest further the argument that denying recovery from the original debtor did not foreclose recovery by the creditor from the state. The creditor would be denied only a "present right" of recovery by a finding for the debtor. Marshall's reference to Vattel suggested further that he used the analogy of the substitution of a hostage to take the place of an initial hostage who, because of a change in status, no longer could be deemed a hostage (a prince who becomes a king) to represent the substitution of the state of Virginia for the original debtor who, by paying into the state treasury, no longer retained the status of debtor.[103] The reference to Vattel also supported the argument that as good faith and the "justly presumed intention of the contracting parties ought to be adhered to" in determining obligations under treaties, the United States and Great Britain had not intended that a debtor should pay his debt twice.[104]

Iredell also wrote, "Payments into the Treasury. . . . Debtor completely discharged—." Marshall insisted that the debtor was completely discharged because he had paid his debt into the state treasury. The debt no longer existed as to the original debtor. The plaintiff, therefore, could not collect. This argument supported the special plea of *nil debit* (do not owe):

> Not Debt if paid off to the Plaintiff—
> Nor if paid in any other manner.
> Same as if Creditor had received payment—
> Impediment by law—not by fact—
> Payment a fact its operation by law lawful discharge.[105]

Marshall argued that his client had paid his debt into the state treasury and that he was not a *bona fide* debtor under the treaty. He reasoned that his client had been discharged and that this posed a factual impediment to recovery, not a legal impediment proscribed by the treaty. By arguing that the debt posed a factual discharge, counsel apparently hoped to avoid having the state sequestration act declared unconstitutional by the effect of the supremacy clause in the Constitution.

When the case was argued May 29, 1793, Associate Justice Iredell, Chief Justice John Jay, and District Judge Griffin heard the arguments. They unanimously struck down all of the defense special pleas except the defense of payment into the loan office. Jay voted to strike this defense also, but Iredell and Griffin held that payment under the sequestration act discharged the individual debtor. They reasoned that the law of nations dictated a general right of confiscation that sanctioned Virginia's sequestration act. The creditor's recourse, accordingly, should be against the state as sequestration did not work a complete confiscation. Jay found that the treaty annulled the act, but he reasoned additionally that the sequestration act that provided for voluntary compliance placed the act outside the customary law of nations regarding confiscation.[106]

These rulings left open for decision only the loan office plea, which came up before the Supreme Court on appeal in February 1796. The case was heard by Justices Samuel Chase, William Paterson, James Wilson, and William Cushing. The decision confirmed Jay's opinion that payment to the loan office did not discharge the debtor. Justice Iredell, "in conformity to a practice . . .

forebore taking any part in [the] decision, as a judge. But he observed, that he thought there would be no impropriety in his reading in his place the reasons he had given in support of the judgment in circuit court."[107]

Marshall argued before the Supreme Court that the sequestration act barred recovery because Virginia, as an independent nation, had the general power of confiscating enemy property according to the laws of war. His only reported reference to the international law authorities was a reference to Vattel. "The rights of war clearly exist between members of the same Empire, engaged in a civil war. Vatt. B. 3, s. 292, 295."[108] Under Vattel's analysis, the belligerents in a civil war are equals subject to the "common laws of war."[109] Marshall argued further that "[t]his act of Virginia must have been known to the American and British commissioners, and, therefore, [it could not] be repealed without plain and explicit expressions directed to that object."[110]

Marshall's reliance on logic dictated that he discuss the nature of confiscation. Interestingly, considering Marshall's reputation for honoring property as sacred, he argued that "property is the creature of civil society [not a consequence of natural law] and subject, in all respects to the disposition and controul of civil institutions." He reasoned "that the law of property, in its origin and operation, is the offspring of the social state; not the incident of a state of nature."[111] He thus subjected property to the will of the state. He attempted to answer Jay's reasoning that Virginia's sequestration act was not confiscatory because not obligatory by insisting that although the state "thought proper . . . only to authorize the payment, to exonerate the debtor from his creditor," the "arrangement," when made, was "confiscatory in nature."[112] He asked, "What is confiscation? The substance, and not the form, is to be regarded. The state had a right either to make the confiscation absolute, or to modify it as she pleased."[113]

Marshall and his co-counsel ushered the test case against the British debts through the federal court system to its final conclusion. The Supreme Court decided the case in favor of treaty supremacy, but a lively debate about the power of confiscation in an international law context resulted in defining the law in this area. In his *Commentaries on American Law* published in 1826, James Kent summarized the international law of confiscation as it had developed.

> Down to the year 1737, the general opinion of jurists was in favour of the right; but Vattel says, that a relaxation of the rigour of the rule has since taken place among the sovereigns of Europe. . . .There has frequently been a stipulation in modern treaties, that debts should not be confiscated in the event of war; and these conventional provisions are evidence of the sense of the governments which are parties to them, and that the right of

> confiscation of debts and things in action is against good policy, and ought to be discontinued.[114]

Kent discussed the modern arguments against allowing confiscation of debts, noting particularly the very able discussions of Alexander Hamilton in the "numbers of *Camillus*," published in defense of Jay's Treaty,[115] but he concluded, "Notwithstanding the weight of modern authority, and of argument, against this claim of right on the part of the sovereign, to confiscate the debts and funds of the subjects of his enemy during war, the judicial language in this country is decidedly in support of the right."[116] Relying on John Marshall's Supreme Court opinion in *Brown v. United States* (1814)[117] that the "right of the sovereign to confiscate debts, was precisely the same with the right to confiscate other property found in the country," Kent continued:

> We, may, therefore, lay it down as a principle of public law, so far as the same is understood and declared by the highest judicial authorities in this country, that it rests in the discretion of the legislature of the Union, by a special law for that purpose, to confiscate debts contracted by our citizens, and due to the enemy; but as asserted by the same authority, this right is contrary to universal practice, and it may, therefore, well be considered as a naked and impolitic right, condemned by the enlightened conscience and judgement of modern times.[118]

Citing John Marshall's decision in *Brown v. United States* (1814), Henry Wheaton, in his 1836 treatise on international law, described the state of the law of confiscation. The right of the "Sovereign to confiscate debts is precisely the same with the right to confiscate other property found within the country on the breaking out of war. Both require some special act expressing the sovereign will, and both depend, not on any inflexible rule of international law, but on political considerations by which the judgment of the Sovereign may be guided."[119]

The sovereign will of the nation during the British debt dispute could not be expressed by the acts of the Virginia state legislature. Treaty provisions took precedence under the supremacy clause. In the *Brown* case, Marshall found that Congress had the "power of confiscating enemy property" (including debts) but had not sufficiently declared "its will to confiscate property within [its jurisdiction] at the declaration of war."[120] The declaration of war itself was not enough.

## ON THE COURT

The issues involving pre-Revolutionary War debts that came before the Supreme Court while Marshall was Chief Justice did not involve the constitutional and political issues settled by *Ware* in 1796 and through international diplomacy in 1802. The legal right to collect debts could no longer be defended by pleading payment under the various sequestration and confiscation acts. The *Ware* decision had settled the matter for the courts. Marshall, however, wrote opinions in several cases in which the understanding and knowledge gained from the British debt issue served him well. Some of these cases came to the Court under Virginia law.

The case, *Dunlop v. Ball* (1804), involved a debt contracted in 1773 by a Virginia debtor with a British creditor.[121] The note was secured by a bond executed on the same date. The debtor defended that more than twenty years had elapsed before the creditor pursued his rights, giving rise to the legal presumption of payment. The creditor contended that legal impediments imposed by various state acts had prevented him from bringing suit and that twenty years, exclusive of the period of legal disability, had not elapsed. The case could have been determined simply by counting the time in which the creditor could have sued to determine if twenty years had passed, but the jury in the lower court had not been instructed to consider the possibility of legal impediments. As the presumption that the creditor was dilatory in pursuing his claim could be outweighed by considering facts not before the jury, Marshall remanded the case to be tried on these issues.

In another case of similar import, a question was certified to the Court for an opinion on the effect of the various acts on the statute of limitations and a British debt. In *Hopkirk v. Bell* (1806), the Fifth Circuit Court certified the question,[122] "Whether the act of assembly of Virginia for the limitation of actions pleaded by the defendant was, under all the circumstances stated, a bar to the plaintiff's demand founded on a promissory note . . . of the 2lst day of August, 1773?"[123] Marshall objected to hearing the question, no doubt, because it purported to cover all circumstances and involved fact determinations for the jury. The Court returned the opinion that the time before the war was not to be counted within the limitation period.

In *Higginson v. Mein* (1808), Marshall again looked at the statute of limitation in relation to the debt issue.[124] A creditor sued a bondsman on a note contracted with a loyal British subject who chose to fight with the British and returned to Britain during the war. Marshall reasoned that the statutory impediments that could have the effect of extending the statute of limitations could not apply in the case, but remanded the case for trial of any other extenuating circumstances.

Clearly, these three cases did not require Marshall to use extensive knowledge of international law. But in cases with questions of confiscation, as in the *Brown* case, Marshall was required to apply his knowledge to determine the right of confiscation of enemy property during time of war. Cases in the period preceding, during, and following the War of 1812, involving property belonging to merchants domiciled in foreign countries presented the Court with mixed questions of confiscation and citizenship. Interestingly, the question of citizenship was also discussed in *Ware v. Hylton*. Justice Chase, delivering the opinion for the Court, noted, "On the declaration of independence, it was in the option of any subject of Great Britain, to join their brethren in America, or to remain subjects of Great Britain."[125] Merchants with foreign domiciles were often also confronted with the problem of choosing loyalties or of having the court choose for them. Confiscation of merchant goods was more direct and immediate than confiscation of debts. For the right of confiscation to arise, however, the property to be confiscated had to be enemy goods.

The following three cases illustrate Marshall's grasp of the law of confiscation and his resolution of the issue of citizenship involved in the cases. The opinions also indicate that Marshall did not subscribe completely to the doctrine of perpetual allegiance.

In *The Venus* (1814),[126] Marshall filed a long and impassioned dissent to the portion of the majority opinion written by Justice Bushrod Washington ascribing expatriation to a merchant living in England at the outbreak of hostilities during the War of 1812. A United States citizen with a commercial domicile in a foreign country on whom his native country had declared war, Marshall argued, had, by the law of nations and natural justice, a reasonable amount of time to return to his country. He also noted that Vattel was more "explicit and more satisfactory on [the subject] than any other whose work ha[d] fallen into [his] hands."[127]

Four merchants—Maitland, McGregor, Lenox and Jones—were naturalized American citizens, engaged actively in commercial trade between the United States and England with commercial houses in both countries. When war was declared, McGregor and Lenox were living in the United States, Jones was living in England. Maitland, in England, sought to return to the United States. *The Venus* was registered to Lenox and Maitland, whereas the cargo was variously designated as the property of the four men. Both cargo and vessel were libeled for prize as enemy property. The majority held that *The Venus* was enemy property, being registered to Maitland, who, living in England, was declared expatriated. Marshall, in dissenting, insisted that an American with "merely a commercial domicil in a foreign country" should not be precluded "from averring and proving an intention to change his domicil on the breaking out of war."[128] To the possibility that such a person would automatically be "clothed with the character of an enemy," Marshall declared, "[m]y sense of justice revolts from such a principle."[129] Marshall insisted, relying on Burlemaque, that the merchant should have "reasonable time to retire."[130]

Marshall's language in *Murray v. The Charming Betsy* (1804),[131] as well as his holding in the case, implicitly recognized the right of expatriation. He noted, however, that the Court was not deciding "Whether a person born within the United States, or becoming a citizen according to the established laws of the country, [could] divest himself absolutely of that character otherwise than in such manner as may be prescribed by law."[132]

Jared Shattuck, although born in the United States, had been taken as an infant to St. Thomas. He lived there most of his life, married and acquired property there, and took the oath of allegiance to the crown of Denmark in 1797. He "carried on trade as a Danish subject." His ship, *The Charming Betsy*, was taken by the French as prize but was recaptured by *The Constellation*, commanded by Captain Murray, who, treating the vessel as an American ship, libeled it in Philadelphia under the non-intercourse law that prohibited United States citizens from trading with France. The Consul of Denmark claimed the ship as property of a Danish subject. Marshall found that Shattuck was a Danish burgher and assessed damages against the recaptor, Murray, to be paid by the United States. He reasoned:

> The American citizen who goes into a foreign country, although he owes local and temporary allegiance to that country, is yet, if he performs no other act changing his condition, entitled to the protection of his own government; . . . But his situation is completely changed, where by his own act he has made himself the subject of a foreign power. Although this act may not be sufficient to rescue him from punishment for any crime committed against the United States,[133] a point not intended to be decided, yet it certainly places him out of the protection of the United States while within the territory of the sovereign to whom he has sworn allegiance.[134]

Marshall thus qualified expatriation, intimating (but not deciding) that the native country may retain penal authority over the person naturalized. He narrowly defined Shattuck's citizenship, relying in essence on Shattuck's decision to become a Danish citizen. The effect, however, was complete. *The Charming Betsy* was held not to be subject to recapture, and charges were assessed against the libelant, Captain Murray, who had commanded *The Constellation*. The clerk noted at the end of the decision that the captain was "reimbursed his damages, interest and charges out of the treasury of the United States, by an act of Congress, January 31, 1805."[135] The report of the arguments in the case included a full discussion of the state of the law on the right of expatriation. Although the Supreme Court recognized that Chief Justice Ellsworth in a case before the Circuit Court in Connecticut was reported to have held "that a citizen of the United States could not expatriate himself," the Court "inclined to the opinion that the right exists, but the difficulty was, that the law had not pointed out the mode of election of proof."[136]

In a case heard in 1818, the Court addressed the question of reversion of citizenship to a merchant and, indirectly, the theory of perpetual allegiance. The brig *Friendschaft* was captured by a privateer commissioned by the United States, the *Herald*, brought into Cape Fear, North Carolina, and libeled as war prize.[137] The ship contained numerous goods, a portion of which was claimed by Joseph Winn, a merchant whose house of business was in Portugal, a neutral country, but whose native country was Great Britain.

The lower court reasoned that Winn's place of domicile for commercial purposes was Lisbon, Portugal, and allowed his claim for restitution of his goods. Henry Wheaton, counsel for the captors, urged the Court to reverse and find that Winn's nationality was British and his goods therefore subject to condemnation. He relied on Sir William Scott for the authority that British subjects resident in Portugal retained their citizenship. He also argued that Winn's citizenship reattached when he returned to England.[138] Marshall rejected the arguments. He held that the claimant's business was in Portugal and that he intended to return to Portugal, although he had gone to England on business. He noted that the privileges enjoyed by British subjects in Portugal were "very great; but, . . . they do not confound the British and Portuguese character. They do not identify the two nations with each other, or affect those principles on which, in other cases, a merchant acquires the character of the nation in which he resides and carries on his trade." Marshall also stated his reasons for deciding the issue strictly on the exception to perpetual allegiance, the commercial domicile rule: "If a British merchant, residing in Portugal, retains his British character while Britain is at war and Portugal at peace, he would also retain that character when Portugal is at war and Britain at peace. This no belligerent could tolerate. Its effect would be to neutralize the whole commerce of Portugal, and give it perfect security."[139]

Marshall declined to state, in the cases before him, his complete views on expatriation. In *The Venus* he endorsed, relying on international law, the right of a merchant living abroad to choose his place of domicile at the outbreak of hostilities. In *Murray v. The Charming Betsy*, he indicated that certain acts could effect expatriation. In *The Friendschaft*, he held that the temporary domicile acquired by merchants in foreign countries was stronger than a theory of perpetual allegiance would imply. He also denounced the logic of dual citizenship. Marshall also endorsed the practice of naturalization, which required as the first step that one renounce his prior allegiance. As a member of the House of Delegates, he had taken the official oath in which he "relinquish[ed] and renounce[d] the Character of Subject or citizen of any Prince or other State whatsoever, and abjure[d] all allegiance which may be claimed by such Prince or other State."[140] Significantly, Marshall decided the cases involving confiscation and citizenship strictly. He did not indulge in his tendency to engage in *obiter dictum*, he applied the law of nations as he understood it. Marshall recognized exceptions and qualifications to the rigid doctrine of perpetual allegiance, and in so doing, helped to weaken the doctrine.

Ziegler concludes in his work on John Marshall and international law,[141] as did Beveridge before him,[142] that Marshall endorsed the principle of perpetual allegiance and denied the right of expatriation. As evidence of Marshall's opinion, Ziegler relies on a letter Marshall wrote Timothy Pickering, former Secretary of State. Marshall thanked Pickering for sending a copy of a pamphlet written by John Lowell, a Massachusetts lawyer, and expressed agreement with the contents. Lowell reviewed and criticized a government sponsored pamphlet written by George Hay, a Virginia lawyer, justifying impressment as a cause for war.[143] Lowell also evaluated the status of the law of expatriation under the "Modern Usage of Nations," and asserted that "if any one nation maintain[ed] the doctrine of perpetual allegiance, every other nation [was] bound to respect her claims over her own subjects."[144] The two pamphlets presented a thorough review of the history of the law of perpetual allegiance and the concurrent issues of emigration, naturalization and expatriation, and were in essence legal briefs on the subject. Both referred extensively to treatises on the law of nations and Lowell ably reviewed the existing law. Marshall's approval of the Lowell pamphlet did not, as Ziegler suggests, prove that he was lost "in the vast field of international law" without "the guiding hands of the more learned counsel in the profession to lead him."[145] Marshall's endorsement indicates that he had a broad understanding of the international law involved in the dispute and that he agreed with Lowell's political views.[146]

Although Marshall, as counsel, approached the debt issue in *Ware* in the narrow context of a creditor-debtor problem, he was forced by the nationality of the parties, the intervening war, and the treaty provisions controlling Virginia state laws to use principles of international law. Out of the dispute, the constitutional principle of the supremacy of treaty was articulated, but broader questions of confiscation of enemy property and the underlying questions of citizenship were explored as was the effect of a declaration of war on enemy goods. During this period, the general rule of the law of nations that sanctioned the belligerent's absolute right of confiscation of enemy goods was subject to change through treaty agreements as well as through custom. International commerce necessitated an amelioration of the more rigid rule. Marshall's experiences in the test case and in the debate over the Jay Treaty allowed him to reach informed decisions on the issues while exploring and applying the principles of international law.

The central issue in the debt cases—payment of pre-revolutionary debts to British subjects—offered Marshall a unique opportunity. The arguments in *Ware* were fashioned to reconcile the fact of non-payment with the 1783 peace treaty provisions. Marshall argued that the treaty had been mutually broken or that the proper debtor was the state. He did not deny that the treaty provisions controlled, he sought to reconcile the provisions to his client's case. Later, he endorsed the solution through arbitration provided in the Jay Treaty, preferring arbitration by a commission with well-defined jurisdiction to the lump-sum solution eventually reached. The arbitration provisions in the Jay Treaty had lasting implications in international law. The Jay Treaty with its arbitration provisions in Articles V, VI, and VII[147] marked the beginning of the modern era of arbitration. Marshall personally endorsed the concept and worked publicly to support it, evidencing a mature understanding of the matrix of international law.

## NOTES

1. 8 Cranch 110 (1814).
2. 8 Cranch 110, 154.
3. 3 Dallas 199 (1796).
4. *Ibid.*, p. 112.
5. 8 Cranch 110, 128.
6. *Ibid.*, p. 124.
7. *Ibid.*, p. 123.
8. Hunter Miller, ed., *Treaties and Other International Acts of the United States of America, 1776-1863*, 8 vols. (Washington, D.C., 1931-1948), vol. 2, p. 154.
9. While Chief Justice, Marshall ruled in another British debt case in which he applied constitutional supremacy to the peace treaty. In *Hopkirk v. Bell*, 3 Cranch 454, 4 Cranch 164 (1806), a case certified to the Supreme Court, the court ruled that the Virginia state statute of limitation could not be used to impede debt collection. Specifically, the Court found that pre-revolutionary time could not be counted to compute the statute of limitation and that British merchants were protected by a savings clause in the act that applied to foreigners. *See supra*, discussion of case at p. 32.
10. For a discussion of the differences in the developing public and private law in the fifty years following the Revolution, see George Dargo, *Law in the New Republic: Private Law and the Public Estate* (New York: Alfred A. Knopf, Inc., 1983), p. 7 et seq.
11. The essays were published in the *Virginia Gazette and General Advertiser*. Marshall's pro-administration views were expressed in four essays published on September 8, October 16, November 13, and November 20. In the essay of November 13, Marshall, under the pseudonym of "Gracchus," discussed the British debt issue. Historian Harry Ammon accepts Marshall's authorship of the four essays. See "Agricola Versus Aristides: James Monroe, John Marshall, and the Genêt Affair in Virginia," *The Virginia Magazine of History and Biography* 74 (July 1966): 312-20. Biographer Leonard Baker, after examining the essays, decided that they lacked internal consistency. He concludes that the "Gracchus" letters were written by Marshall but that "another Richmond Federalist" wrote the two "Aristedes [*sic*]" letters. He bases his conclusions on the "sound" of the letters and admits that whether "Marshall was one or both is unknown, although he was undoubtedly intimately involved in their preparation." Baker, *John Marshall: A Life in Law*, pp. 197-200. Ammon relies on contemporary acceptance of the authorship as one and notes that two signatures were used because each dealt with different "aspects of the controversy." Ammon, "Agricola Versus Aristides," p. 313. Both men agree that Marshall wrote the letter on November 13 discussing the British debt issue.
12. Cullen and Johnson, eds., *The Papers of John Marshall*, vol. 2,

pp. 196-200. Marshall headed the committee that drafted the resolutions reflecting these sentiments that were published in the *Virginia Gazette and General Advertiser* on August 21, in the *Maryland Journal* on August 27 and in the *Maryland Gazette* on August 29. Similar meetings were held in other states.

13. Philip Marsh, "James Monroe as 'Agricola' in the Genêt Controversy, 1793," *Virginia Magazine of History and Biography* 62 (October 1954): 472-76.

14. Norman K. Risjord, *Chesapeake Politics* (New York: Columbia University Press, 1978), p. 84.

15. *Ibid.*, p. 135.

16. John Marshall to Augustine Davis, September 11, 1793, in Cullen and Johnson, eds., *The Papers of John Marshall*, vol. 2, p. 202.

17. *Ibid.*, Marshall to Augustine Davis, November 13, 1793, vol. 2, pp. 232-33.

18. *Ibid.*, p. 233.

19. *Ibid.*, p. 234.

20. John Marshall, *The Life of George Washington* (New York: Chelsea House, 1986 <1805>), vol. 5, pp. 70-71.

21. *Ibid.*, p. 71.

22. Marshall to Story, December 25, 1932.

23. *Ibid.*

24. William Waller Hening, ed., *The Statutes at Large . . . of Virginia . . .* 13 vols. (Richmond, Philadelphia, and New York, 1809-23), vol. 11, pp. 75-76.

25. Richard B. Morris, ed., *John Jay: The Winning of the Peace: Unpublished Papers, 1780-1784* (New York: Harper & Row, 1980), pp. 385-86.

26. *Ibid.*, p. 414.

27. *Ibid.*, p. 396.

28. *Ibid.*, p. 429. Townshend and the Cabinet were disappointed in Oswald's performance in Paris, specifically considering him "too easy" on the debt issue. See Richard Morris, *The Peacemakers* (New York: Harper and Row, Publishers, 1965), p. 352.

29. *Ibid.*, p. 441.

30. *Ibid.*, Livingston to Commissioners, March 25, 1783, p. 520.

31. *Ibid.*, pp. 556-57. Jefferson, answering on January 24, 1786, questions propounded by Monsieur de Meusnier, author of *Encyclopedie Politique* about British property after the war, noted the economic difficulties attending payment of the debts:

> The states differed very much in their proceedings as to British property; and I am unable to give the details. In Virginia, the sums sequestered in the treasury remain precisely as they did at the conclusion of the peace. The British having refused to make satisfaction for the slaves they carried away, contrary to the

> treaty of peace, and to deliver up the posts within our limits, the execution of that treaty is in some degree suspended. Individuals however are paying off their debts to British subjects, and the laws even permit the latter to recover them judicially. But as the amount of these debts are 20 to 30 times the amount of all the money in circulation in that state, the same laws permit the debtor to pay his debt in seven equal & annual payments.

Paul Leicester Ford, ed., *The Works of Thomas Jefferson* (New York: G. P. Putnam's Sons, 1904), vol. 5, pp. 17-18.

32. Morris, *John Jay: The Winning of the Peace*, p. 547.

33. *Journal of the House of Delegates of the Commonwealth of Virginia*, May 3, 1784, session (Richmond, Thomas W. White, Opposite the Bell-Tavern, 1828), p. 41.

34. Complaints against British non-compliance with the terms of peace would increase and would become a standard defense used by debtors to defeat collection. John Marshall with other Virginia lawyers incorporated the complaint into one of the special defense pleas used in the test case, *Ware v. Hylton et al.* and pleaded most eloquently by Patrick Henry.

35. *Journal of the House of Delegates of the Commonwealth of Virginia*, May 3, 1784, p. 41.

36. Johnson, ed., *The Papers of John Marshall*, vol. 1, p. 130, n. 7. See also Emory Evans,"Private Indebtedness and the Revolution in Virginia, 1776 to 1796," *William and Mary Quarterly*, 3d ser., 28 (1971), pp. 349-374.

37. Johnson, ed., *The Papers of John Marshall*, vol. 1, p. 130.

38. *Dunlop and Co. v. Ball*, 2 Cranch 180, 6 U.S. 180 (1804). Marshall delivered the opinion that remanded to the lower court for a fact determination on the statute of limitation. See discussion *infra*, p. 32.

39. 2 Cranch 180, 181-82.

40. Charles Hobson, an editor of *The Marshall Papers*, refutes the "standard" historical view that "the constitution and the creation of a federal court system secured the interests of the creditors." See Charles F. Hobson, "The Recovery of British Debts in the Federal Circuit Court of Virginia, 1790 to 1797," *The Virginia Magazine of History and Biography* 92, no. 2 (April 1984). See also Evans, "Private Indebtedness," *William and Mary Quarterly*, 3d ser., 27 (1971), p. 349.

41. 3 Dallas 199, 199-200.

42. Jefferson was familiar with the debt issue as he was governor during the time that the loan office accepted payments. On January 24, 1786, he estimated the value of Virginia's debt to be two millions sterling, noting that some "conjectured the debt as high as three millions. I think [Virginia] owed near as much as all the rest put together. This is to be ascribed to peculiarities in the tobacco trade." Paul Leicester Ford, *The Works of Thomas Jefferson* (New York: G. P. Putnam's Sons, 1904), vol. 5, "Answers to Questions Propounded by M. de Meusnier," p. 28.

43. Although Jefferson usually stressed that the debts were being paid, he noted in 1786, "On our part we have not paid our debts, and it will take time to pay them. In conferences with some distinguished mercantile characters, I found them sensible of the impossibility of our paying these debts at once, and that an endeavor to force universal & immediate paiment would render debts desperate, which are good in themselves." Jefferson to James Ross, May 8, 1786, Ford, ed. *The Works of Thomas Jefferson*, vol. 5, p. 102.

44. Resistance to paying war interest, that is, interest computed during the war years, was strong; although allowed in *Ware v. Hylton et al.*, it was routinely disallowed thereafter. For a summary of the arguments against paying it (including those of Thomas Jefferson), see Charles F. Hobson, ed., *The Papers of John Marshall: Selected Law Cases, 1784-1800* (Chapel Hill: The University of North Carolina Press, 1987), vol. 5, p. 370.

45. Hobson, ed., *The Papers of John Marshall*, vol. 5, pp. 328-29, n. 2.

46. 3 Dallas 199, 213.

47. Ford, ed., *The Works of Thomas Jefferson*, vol. 5, p. 46.

48. Treaty of Amity, Commerce and Navigation; concluded November 19, 1794, ratified in London October, 28, 1795, and proclaimed February 29, 1796.

49. Samuel Flagg Bemis, *Jay's Treaty: A Study in Commerce and Diplomacy* (New York: The Macmillan Company, 1923), p. 326.

50. Albert J. Beveridge, *The Life of John Marshall: Frontiersman, Soldier, Lawmaker: Politician, Diplomatist, Statesman, 1789-1801* (Dunwoody, Ga.: Norman S. Berg, Publisher, 1974), vol. 2, pp. 200-201. Marshall's only debt to a British citizen, Lord Fairfax, was contracted sometime in 1793-1794. *Ibid.*, p. 204.

51. John Bassett Moore, *History and Digest of the International Arbitrations to Which the United States Has Been a Party* (Washington: United States Printing Office, 1898), vol. 1, p. 284.

52. *Ibid.*, p. 290.

53. Cullen, ed., *The Papers of John Marshall*, vol. 4, p. 42.

54. *Ibid.*

55. Bemis, *Jay's Treaty*, p. 318.

56. Cullen, ed., *The Papers of John Marshall*, vol. 4, p. 136.

57. *Ibid.*, Marshall to John Adams, August 12, 1800, p. 215.

58. *Ibid.*, John Adams to John Marshall, August 22, 1800, p. 229, John Marshall to John Adams, August 23, 1800, p. 230.

59. *Ibid.*, John Adams to John Marshall, August 1, 1800, p. 198.

60. *Ibid.*, John Marshall to John Adams, August 16, 1800, p. 224.

61. *Ibid.*, John Marshall to John Adams, August 12, 1800, p. 215.

62. *Ibid.*, John Adams to John Marshall, August 26, 1800, p. 245.

63. *Ibid.*, p. 250.

64. *Ibid.*, John Marshall to Rufus King, August 23, 1800, p. 234.

65. *Ibid.*, p. 238.

66. *Ibid.*, p. 239.

67. Hobson, ed., *The Papers of John Marshall*, vol. 5, p. 263. Samuel Flagg Bemis concludes "The matter was finally left to the American courts, from jurisdiction of which Jay should never have allowed it to escape." Bemis, *Jay's Treaty*, p. 319.

68. Beveridge, *The Life of John Marshall*, vol. 2, p. 505, n. 3.

69. *Ibid.*, p. 200, n. 3.

70. *Ibid.*, p. 502. Rufus King to Secretary of State, April 22, 1800. Cullen, ed., *The Papers of John Marshall*, vol. 4, p. 132.

71. *Ibid.*, John Marshall to Rufus King, August 23, 1800, p. 239.

72. Charles Warren, *The Supreme Court in United States History* (Boston: Little, Brown, and Company, 1926), p. 144.

73. Bemis, *Jay's Treaty*, p. 103. See also Robert Douthat Meade, *Patrick Henry: Practical Revolutionary* (New York: J. B. Lippincott Company,1969), p. 405. The majority of cases filed in Virginia were for the recovery of small sums owed by planters to Scottish factors. See Charles F. Hobson, *The Papers of John Marshall*, vol. 5, p. 376.

74. Moore, *International Arbitrations*, vol. 1, p. 286.

75. Hening, *Statutes*, XI, p. 76.

76. Hobson, ed., *The Papers of John Marshall*, vol. 5, p. 259.

77. U.S. Circuit Court, Va., Ended Cases (Restored), 1797. The case was filed in 1790 and initially heard on November 24, 1791, but there was no ruling in the case as Justice John Blair's son's death necessitated his departure during the arguments. The verdict was finally entered May 27, 1797, on the debt pleaded in the original complaint. The court found for the plaintiff but deducted eight years' interest during the war.

78. Hening, *Statutes*, IX, 377-80.

79. Hening, *Statutes*, X, 67.

80. Hobson, ed., *The Papers of John Marshall*, vol. 5, pp. 284-85.

81. See Hobson, ed., *The Papers of John Marshall*, vol. 5, pp. 273-94, for the complete text of the pleas here summarized to reflect the substance of the arguments.

82. Hobson, ed., *The Papers of John Marshall*, vol. 5, pp. 300-313.

83. *Ibid.*, pp. 317-27.

84. *Ibid.*, pp. 300-13 and 317-27. Ziegler relied only on the published case report and found it significant that Marshall quoted only one authority. Ziegler, *The International Law of John Marshall*, p. 150, n. 143. Arthur Nussbaum, research professor in public law at Columbia University, cautioned against placing too much importance on citations in reported cases as they "are sometimes influenced by extrinsic motives." This seems particularly applicable in this case as the published report was based on *opposing* counsel's notes. Nussbaum, *A Concise History of the Law of Nations*, p. 162.

85. Ziegler, *The International Law of John Marshall*, p. 13.

86. *Ibid.*, p. 16. Ziegler, counting citations in reported cases, found

that Marshall cited only one authority in *Ware* (1796) but, under the guidance of counsel, could cite three in *Brown* (1814). Ziegler also referred Marshall for reinforcement of his own view to the more complete dissent filed by Story in *Brown*.

87. Edward Dumbauld, "John Marshall and the Law of Nations," 104 U. Pa. L. Rev. 39, 40 (1955).

88. Legal training for lawyers consisted at the time primarily of reading under an attorney for a period of time (approximately a year) before taking the state bar examination. In this connection, it is notable that twenty of the twenty-two lawyers who sat on the Bench during Marshall's tenure read under practicing attorneys. None had a formal law degree, although a predecessor, John Rutledge, after reading law in his uncle's office, studied in London's Middle Temple. Olliver Ellsworth formally studied theology but decided to study for the bar on his own. John Blair, Jr., studied law at London's Middle Temple and was admitted to practice upon his return to Virginia. See Leon Friedman & Fred L. Israel, eds., *The Justices of the United States Supreme Court, 1789-1978*, vol 1., pp. 5, 34, 60, 82, 109, 122, 153, 163, 185, 224, 244, 269, 356, 388, 408, 422, 436, 476, 514, 535, 571, 601. Only unverified family legend has Marshall reading under a practicing attorney. Thomas Jefferson advised against reading under an attorney, being of the opinion that "the placing of a youth to study with an attorney was rather a prejudice than a help." Quoted in Edward Dumbauld, *Thomas Jefferson and the Law* (Norman: University of Oklahoma Press, 1978), p. 7. He advised his future son-in-law to spend his time wisely—alone with law books. "All the aid you will want will be a catalogue of the books to be read and the order in which to read them." *Ibid.*, p. 164, n. 17. A recent corrective of Jefferson's training appears in Frank L. Dewey's *Thomas Jefferson, Lawyer*, (Charlottesville: University Press of Virginia, 1986). Jefferson reportedly had studied law at William and Mary for five years. Dewey shows that Jefferson began studying law under Wythe in 1762, continued reading at Shadwell during 1763, and spent the next two years sporadically studying and training in Williamsburg. Oliver Wendell Holmes was the first justice with a formal legal degree to sit on the Supreme Court. Although all of the first one hundred justices were lawyers, it was "not until March 25, 1957, that all nine members of the Supreme Court were law school graduates." Albert P. Blaustein and Roy M. Mersky, *The First One Hundred Justices: Statistical Studies on the Supreme Court of the United States* (Hamden, Conn.: Shoe String Press, Inc., 1978), pp. 20-21.

89. William Wirt, *Sketches of the Life and Character of Patrick Henry* (New York: Derby & Jackson, 1857), p. 329.

90. *Ibid.*, p.340.

91. *Ibid.*, p. 344.

92. *Ibid.*, p. 360.

93. *Ibid.*, p. 346.

94. *Ibid.*, p. 348.

95. *Ibid.*, p. 347.

96. *Ibid.*, p. 353.

97. *Ibid.*, p. 360.

98. Hobson, ed., *The Papers of John Marshall*, vol. 5, p. 267.

99. *Ibid.*, p. 300.

100. *Ibid.*, p. 302.

101. *Ibid.*, p. 303.

102. *Ibid.*, p. 305.

103. The citation in the Iredell notes is correct under this analysis. In Book II, Vattel deals with the observance of treaties, and in section 257, he discusses the consequences to the parties of a treaty when a prince "given in hostage, succeeds to the crown." Marshall found an arguable equivalent in the law of nations to the concept of substitution of parties or subrogation or assignment in municipal law, a concept that supported Marshall's arguments. Emmerich de Vattel, *The Law of Nations, or Principles of the Law of Nature, applied to the Conduct and Affairs of Nations and Sovereigns* (London, G. G. and J. Robinson, Paternoster-Row, 1797), Book II, § 257, p. 242. The editors of *The Papers of John Marshall* suggest that the citation is incorrect and that the reference should have been to Book III, § 257, which deals with the right of belligerents during a period of truce to allow or disallow enemy access to the belligerent country. Hobson, ed., *The Papers of John Marshall*, vol. 5, p. 305, n. 41. Apparently, the citation is correct as noted.

104. Vattel, *The Law of Nations*, Book II, § 257, p. 242.

105. *Ibid.*, p. 306.

106. *Federal Cases [1789-1880]*, 30 vols.(St. Paul, 1874-1897), XIII, no. 7, 507, 1064-69. For a discussion of Jay's surviving Circuit Court opinion, see Charles F. Hobson, "The Recovery of British Debts in the Federal Circuit Court of Virginia, 1790 to 1797", *The Virginia Magazine of History and Biography* 92:176, 189, n.36.

107. 3 Dallas 199, 256, n. 1.

108. 3 Dallas 199, 211. Ziegler thought that this referenced an insignificant point. Virginia's right to confiscate enemy property was, however, central to Marshall's defense. The fact that opposing counsel noted only this reference reveals more about the defense than about Marshall's understanding of international law. Ziegler, *The International Law of John Marshall*, p. 150, n. 143.

109. Vattel, *The Law of Nations*, Book III, §§ 292-95, pp. 424-27.

110. 3 Dallas 199, 214.

111. 3 Dallas 199, 211.

112. 3 Dallas 199, 212.

113. *Ibid.*

114. Kent, *Commentaries on American Law*, vol. 1, p.60.

115. The thirty-eight essays written by Hamilton and Rufus King under the pseudonym of "Camillus" and published in the *New York Argus* beginning on July 22, 1795, endorsed the Jay Treaty. They represented the Federalists'

view but "did not allay the determination of Republican leaders to abort implementation of the treaty." Jacob Ernest Cooke, *Alexander Hamilton* (New York: Charles Scribner's Sons, 1982), p. 164. See also Gilbert L. Lycan, *Alexander Hamilton & American Foreign Policy: A Design for Greatness* (Norman: University of Oklahoma Press, 1970), pp. 226-55.

116. *Ibid.*, p. 61.

117. 8 Cranch 123 (1814)

118. Kent, *Commentaries*, p. 62.

119. Wheaton, *Elements of International Law*, p. 357.

120. 8 Cranch 110, 129. But see Justice Story's strong dissent, considering the declaration of war a sufficient manifestation of intention to confiscate enemy property.

121. 2 Cranch 180 (1804).

122. 3 Cranch 454 (1806).

123. *Ibid.*

124. 4 Cranch 415 (1808).

125. 3 Dallas 199, at 225.

126. 8 Cranch 253 (1814).

127. 8 Cranch 253, 289.

128. *Ibid.*, p. 315.

129. *Ibid.*, p. 315.

130. *Ibid.*, p. 292.

131. 2 Cranch 64 (1804).

132. 2 Cranch 64, 120.

133. Marshall was probably referring here to the case of Isaac Williams, who was commissioned an officer in the French navy and served in the French war against the British. Williams, born in the United States, claimed that he had been naturalized in 1792. He was prosecuted as a citizen of the United States for waging war on the British. Chief Justice Ellsworth, sitting on the Circuit Court of Connecticut in 1799, decided the question on the common law, reasoning that citizenship was a "compact" between a "community and its members" that could not be unilaterally broken. The right of self-expatriation was therefore denied, and Williams was convicted for the crime committed against the United States. See text of the opinion reprinted in John E. Hall, ed., *The American Law Journal* (Philadelphia: Sergeant Hall, Printer, 1813), p. 461-63. When Marshall was Secretary of State, at Adams's request, he polled the cabinet and advised that they unanimously approved a pardon for Williams, whereupon Adams issued the pardon, which had been requested by Governor Jonathan Trumbull of Connecticut. Marshall expressed his personal opinion of the case in a letter to St. George Tucker on November 27, 1800. Charles F. Hobson, ed., *The Papers of John Marshall: Correspondence, Papers, and Selected Judicial Opinions November 1800-1807* (Chapel Hill: The University of North Carolina Press, 1990), vol. 6, pp. 23-24. See also Adams to Marshall, August 7, 1800, Marshall to Adams, August 16, 1800, Marshall to Simeon Baldwin, Court Clerk, Cullen, ed., *The*

*Papers of John Marshall*, vol. 4, pp. 207, 223, 225.

134. 2 Cranch 64, 120.

135. *Ibid.*, p. 126.

136. See the discussion at 2 Cranch 64, 82-113. Counsel argued that the right existed and suggested that three circumstances should be required; fitness in point of time, fairness of intent, and publicity of the act.

137. *The Friendschaft*, 3 Wheat 14 (1818).

138. 3 Wheaton 14, 24-25. For an interesting discussion on this question, see John Reeves, "Whether Inhabitants of the United States, born there before the Independence, are, on coming to this Kingdom, to be considered as natural-born subjects?" John E. Hall, ed., *The American Law Journal* (Philadelphia: Jack Maxwell, Printer, 1817), vol. 6, p. 30.

139. 3 Wheaton 14, 24-25.

140. Johnson, *The Papers of John Marshall*, vol. 1, pp. 87-88.

141. Ziegler relies exclusively on Beveridge's report of an episode in which Marshall wrote a letter interpreted as endorsing perpetual allegiance. In the letter, Marshall alluded to the contents of a pamphlet, which is not reproduced or cited specifically. Marshall also referred to an unidentified principle, which Ziegler finds (without specific reference) to be the doctrine of perpetual allegiance. The argument, as presented, is unconvincing, and on a close reading of the political pamphlets and the Marshall letter, is erroneous. Ziegler discusses Marshall's acceptance of the modes of obtaining citizenship and recognizes a connection with expatriation but does not explore the connection. Marshall denied the justification under international law of impressment as a cause for war with Great Britain. He may have accepted Lowell's assertion that of the 20,000 British seamen employed in United States vessels, only approximately 1,000 were naturalized. Ziegler, *The International Law of John Marshall*, p. 97.

142. Albert J. Beveridge, *The Life of John Marshall: Frontiersman, Soldier, Lawmaker: The Building of the Nation, 1815-1835* (Dunwoody, Ga.: Norman S. Berg, Publisher, 1974), vol. 4, pp. 52-54. Beveridge quoted Marshall's endorsement of the Federalist position against the War of 1812. The letter can best be interpreted as a political reaction to the war. The Republicans endorsed the concept that a person could freely change allegiance and thereby renounce all obligations of prior citizenship, and the Federalists refuted the position. Marshall did not accept all of the positions held by the Federalists, but he *was* against the war. England based the practice of impressment, one of the major causes of the War of 1812, on the doctrine of perpetual allegiance. Marshall was, of course, adamantly opposed to the practice of impressment but hoped to solve the issue short of war.

143. George Hay served as United States Attorney for the District of Virginia, having been appointed to the position by President Thomas Jefferson. He prosecuted the case against Aaron Burr. James Monroe's son-in-law and a member of the Republican administration during the War of 1812, he wrote *A Treatise on Expatriation* to present a "correct exposition on the true

doctrine of expatriation," and to contribute "toward the vindication of the opposition made by the United States to the British claim of impressment." George Hay, *A Treatise on Expatriation* (Washington: A. and G. Way, Printers, 1814), pp. 1-2. In the tract, he advocated the unfettered right of expatriation and presented a legal brief to support his position.

144. John Lowell, *Review of a 'Treatise on Expatriation'* (Boston: Russell, Cutler and Company, 1814), p. 24.

145. Ziegler, *The International Law of John Marshall*, p. 97.

146. Marshall's ideas on expatriation were perhaps not fully formed. Nowhere were they fully articulated. John Bassett Moore concluded in 1918 after a thorough search of unpublished diplomatic records that the first Secretary of State to announce the doctrine of expatriation "in its fullest extent" was James Buchanan in an instruction of December 18, 1848 to the American minister in London, George Bancroft. See John Bassett Moore, *The Principles of International Diplomacy* (New York: Harper and Brothers Publishers, 1918), p. 276. On July 27, 1868, Congress passed an act declaring the right of expatriation as a "natural and inherent right of all people." In 1870, Great Britain and the United States signed a Convention to avoid the complications of dual citizenship and Great Britain passed a Naturalization Act the same year providing that when a British citizen became naturalized in a foreign state, he would thereafter be regarded as an alien. See Nissim Bar-Yaacov, *Dual Nationality* (New York: Frederick A. Praeger, Publisher, 1961), pp. 95-115. See also Catheryn Seckler-Hudson, *Statelessness: With Special Reference to the United States (A Study in Nationality and Conflict of Laws* (Washington, D.C.: Digest Press, 1934).

147. Jackson H. Ralston, *International Arbitration from Athens to Locarno* (Stanford University: Stanford University Press, 1929), pp. vii, 191. Article V provided for arbitration of the northeast boundary question involving identification of St. Croix, and Article VII provided for arbitration of claims of United States citizens against Great Britain for illegal captures.

# 3

# Minister to France

Marshall was appointed United States *minister extraordinaire* to France by President Adams on June 5, 1797, during a time when political events and sentiments were decidedly against the the mission. The commission appointing him also named Charles Cotesworth Pinckney of South Carolina and Richard Dana of Massachusetts. Dana refused the commission and was replaced by Elbridge Gerry, also from Massachusetts. When Pinckney received his commission, he was already in Amsterdam, having been rejected by the French as official ambassador to succeed James Monroe. The men were sent to France to negotiate differences growing out of French seizure of United States merchant ships. Under the guise of decrees issued on July 2, 1796, and March 2, 1797, France violated the neutral rights of American ships at random, and particularly those enroute to British ports, by subjecting them to seizure and condemnation. War seemed a real possibility.

Diplomatic relations between the United States and France began deteriorating when France declared war on England in 1793 and the Washington administration adopted a policy of neutrality which the French felt repudiated United States obligations to them under the treaties of 1778. Between 1796 and 1797, American ship owners lost over 340 vessels to French privateers and "over fifty-five million dollars' worth of American property had been destroyed or confiscated under the decrees of the Directory."[1] Adams sought through the special mission to redefine French-American relations, to restore diplomatic harmony, and to assert the sovereignty of the United States.

War between England and France divided the people of the United States along party lines. The Washington administration, particularly after the signing of the Jay Treaty with England in 1794, was perceived to be pro-British, whereas the opposing Republicans were more favorable to the French. Marshall endorsed the administration's policies. The Jay Treaty was unpopular in the United States and was seen in France as a virtual alliance against France.

Marshall was serving in the House of Delegates in Richmond when the United States Senate was secretly debating the Treaty. Virginia Senator Stevens Thomson Mason of Virginia gave a copy of the treaty to the *Philadelphia Aurora*, which published it; and Virginians debated the treaty in county meetings and in the state legislature. In the ensuing debates before the House of Delegates in Virginia, the Federalists defended the treaty through argument and dilatory tactics. During this debate, Marshall presented an impressive argument against precipitous state action, contending that the House of Representatives, exercising appropriate constitutional authority, could refuse to appropriate funds and thereby effectively and constitutionally bring the provisions of the treaty into question.[2] Marshall's reputation as an effective spokesman for the Federalist's policies increased, as did his reputation, among political opponents, for being pro-British. Historian Richard Beeman found that the "fundamental difference" separating the political parties in Virginia "lay in their solutions to the British threat."[3] France, quite naturally, preferred the new party that felt more threatened by England.

Consequently, during the 1796 campaign for the presidency, France showed an inordinate interest in the outcome, favoring Thomas Jefferson whom they perceived, with good reason, to favor France. Adams's policies, the French believed, would be a continuation of the Washington administration. Jefferson's bid for the presidency prompted the French to actively seek his election. His defeat was viewed as a defeat for the French faction in the United States. Marshall shared the Federalist view, which resented both French Minister Edmond C. Genêt's efforts in 1793 to extend United States' obligations to France under the 1778 treaty of alliance and the French efforts to influence the election of 1796 as a violation of the rights of the United States as a neutral and independent nation. Historian Harry Ammon characterized the political climate in the United States as a time when "neutrality in politics [was] virtually impossible. The issues . . . compelled men to take sides."[4] He also noted that "American persistence in adhering to a policy of strict neutrality was incomprehensible to [France,] a nation committed to world revolution."[5]

French foreign policy during the 1790s was dedicated to bringing the pro-French Republican party into power.[6] Recognizing French sentiment, Adams, who had defeated Jefferson's 1796 bid for the presidency, wanted to appoint a prominent Republican to serve on the mission. Adams first offered the job to Jefferson, at the time vice-president, and then to Madison. Each declined. Adams knew that the envoys eventually chosen—Pinckney, Gerry, and Marshall—would find a politically hostile atmosphere in Paris. Both Marshall and Pinckney were dedicated Federalists, although Marshall perceived himself to be above party, dedicated only to preserving the nation's independence.[7] Their politics as well as their mission assured them of a cool reception. Gerry was not yet identified with either party. The envoys, during the course of the negotiations, became divided with Gerry taking a position consistent with the Republicans. Marshall and Pinckney would leave Paris without Gerry.

The political aspects of the mission were closely intertwined with the progress of the informal meetings, which began in early October of 1797, three months after the envoys arrived in Paris, and lasted until June of 1798. The French never formally received the envoys, and the first dispatches sent to Secretary of State Timothy Pickering, when made public, added to the political furor. The reports arrived in the United States on March 4 and 7, 1798. Adams merely reported to Congress that he "saw no possibility of success for the special mission."[8] At the insistence of the Republicans in Congress, Adams released the dispatches on April 3. The dispatches revealed not only that the envoys were refused an official audience, but that, after October, they were also constantly bombarded with requests for money by unnamed unofficial emissaries sent by French Minister for Foreign Affairs Charles Maurice Talleyrand. The mission became known as the "XYZ Affair" because Pickering substituted the initials for the unnamed intermediaries. The political effect of the information benefited the Federalists, galvanizing public opinion behind the envoys and increasing the anti-French sentiment in the country.[9]

A review of Marshall's performance supports the hypothesis that he conducted his duties not only as instructed, "with calm dignity," "simplicity," and "inflexible perseverance,"[10] but also according to his conception of the rights of the United States under the law of nations. Marshall proved also to be a firm negotiator. During the six-month wait for formal recognition, Marshall refused to enter into informal discussions and refused to acquiesce in Gerry's insistence that the ministers say that the complaints of the United States were "founded in mistake."[11] Marshall insisted consistently that the envoys must be formally received as official representatives of an independent neutral sovereign, as the underlying purpose permeating the mission was to preserve the independence and neutrality of the United States.[12] He was frustrated by the reception and believed that it was politically motivated. He noted in his journal during the first month of the mission that "Mr. Bellamy, speaking without interruption for near an hour" informed the envoys, "You ought to know that the diplomatic skill of France & the means she possesses in your country are sufficient to enable her with the french party in America to throw the blame which will attend the rupture of the negotiations on the federalists as you term yourself & on the british party as France terms you."[13] The envoys responded that the French "miscalculated on the parties in America. That the extreme injustice offerd to our country would unite every man against her."[14]

Marshall's journal entries, late in the mission, returned to the same theme. Pierre A. Caron de Beaumarchais, one of Talleyrand's intermediaries and Marshall's client in an unresolved suit against Virginia for a war debt, met with Marshall on March 14, 1798, and informed him that the French government believed that the ministers' "refusal to comply with the demands of France was attributable" to Marshall, whom they considered "entirely English."[15] Marshall protested that "neither the government nor any man in France thought [him] English, but they knew [he] was not French: they knew [he] would not sacrifice duty & the interests of [his] own country to any nation on earth."[16]

Marshall tended to equate his understanding of his country's good with the Federalists' vision. Political rhetoric, endorsing this vision, accompanied his return to the United States. It was explicit in the report of the festivities welcoming him home to Richmond, Virginia, on August 8, 1798. As the parade marched by,

> the neighboring citizens came in all directions, to behold the defender of their common rights. . . . In fine, the joy of the day was of so infectious a nature, that each patriotic bosom caught the generous contagion, until the glow of enthusiasm became as general as it was laudable. When future generations shall peruse the history of America, they will find the name of Marshall on its sacred page, as one of the brightest ornaments of the age in which he lived.
>
> Behold him, Virginians! as the unsuccessful messenger of PEACE! After having, in conformity to his instructions and according to the will of his country "drained" (in the language of Washington) "the last drop of the cup of reconciliation"—he has returned to confirm the intelligence, that nothing short of national degradation will be received by the Directory as the price of accommodation—or rather, as the preliminary to negotiation.[17]

When Marshall thanked the cavalry troop, the mayor, recorder, aldermen, and common council of Richmond for the honors bestowed upon him, he expressed "the firm and deep conviction that accommodations with the French Republic on terms consistent with the independence of the United States" had been impracticable and that peace was "unattainable by any just and honorable means."[18]

The failure of the peace mission cannot be ascribed completely to the politics of the two Federalists. The correspondence of the Minister of Foreign Affairs Talleyrand revealed that he in fact intended to postpone substantive negotiations by making demands on the envoys for a bribe, a loan, and apologies for the sentiments expressed in President Adams's May 16, 1797, speech. Talleyrand's object was twofold, to avoid war by prolonging negotiations and to insist that the United States live up to the 1778 treaty obligations.[19] Marshall's refusal to discuss the issues informally and to insist that

France recognize in some degree the public character of the ministers was consistent with his conviction that he represented an equal, independent nation.

William Stinchcombe, diplomatic historian, concluded that the special mission was beneficial, for by "July, 1798, the French had dropped their bribery and loan demands, and an order had been issued calling for cessation of attacks on American vessels." Talleyrand's tactics were costly, but not fatal to a French-American rapprochement.[20] Although Gerry remained in France as the one minister somewhat acceptable to France, his singular attempts to negotiate proved also futile.

The United States during the next two years waged an undeclared limited naval war against France. When Talleyrand, through William Vans Murray, the American minister at The Hague, made known France's willingness to officially negotiate a peace, Adams, digging "his own political grave,"[21] appointed a new commission composed of Chief Justice Oliver Ellsworth, William Vans Murray, and William Richardson Davie. The second commission treated with Napoleon and signed the Treaty of Mortefontaine on September 30, 1800.[22] Marshall was Secretary of State when the treaty was signed. Beveridge noted that the Republicans made "much political capital out of the second mission," claiming to have forced Adams to send the mission to save the United States from war.[23] Under the new treaty, the United States rid itself of all obligations under the treaty of 1778, but gave up claims for injuries done to American commerce. The United States also agreed to pay for damage done to French ships during the Quasi-War. The Federalists complained that the country had "abandon[ed]" its rights and had been "duped" by the French, but Marshall, although "far . . . from approving the treaty," nevertheless recommended ratification.[24]

Thomas Jefferson, as president, used the political aspects of the first mission when he wrote in 1802 to his friend, Pierre Samuel du Pont de Nemours, to enlist his help in the attempt to purchase the Louisiana territory. He added:

> There is another service you can render. I am told that Talleyrand is personally hostile to us. This I suppose, has been occasioned by the XYZ history. But he should consider that that was the artifice of a party, willing to sacrifice him to the consolidation of their power: That this nation has done him justice by dismissing them; that those in power [now], are precisely those who disbelieved that story, and saw in it nothing but an attempt to deceive our country: that we entertain towards him personally the most friendly dispositions; that as to the government of France, we know too little of the state of things there, to understand what it is, and have no inclination to meddle in their settlement.[25]

Marshall's subsequent correspondence reveals that his interpretation of the mission, and of French-American relations, had not softened with time: "All who were then old enough to notice the public affairs of the United States, recollect the arduous struggle of 1798-1799. Genl. Washington, it is well known, took a deep interest in it. He believed that the real independence, the practical self government of our country, depended greatly on its issue—on our resisting the encroachments of France."[26]

Marshall did not perceive the mission to France to be a struggle for power between two contending political parties. To him, it was a struggle for national survival. Marshall joined the diplomatic mission to France because of the pressing need to assert effective national sovereignty. His experiences on the Continent reinforced this conviction.

The mission to France can be understood best by examining the primary sources describing the event. Marshall's writings during this period provide not only his conception of the mission but also the most complete firsthand analysis of the problems encountered by the special envoys. The writings may be divided into four categories.

1. Both Allen B. Magruder and Henry J. Ford, in their respective biographies of Marshall and Timothy Pickering, credit Marshall with authorship of the instructions issued by the State Department.[27] The instructions expressed the administration's view of the rights of the United States under the law of nations.

2. Marshall kept a journal of the events from October 4, 1797, through April 11, 1798, which provides a chonological narrative of the mission.

3. In letters written to Secretary of State Pickering, George Washington, and Attorney General Charles Lee in the United States, Marshall expressed considered but unofficial opinions of the diplomatic events in Paris.

4. Finally, the most complete legal analysis of the envoys' position is contained in the memoranda addressed to Talleyrand written by Marshall.

Collectively, these writings support the hypothesis that Marshall's experiences in international affairs in the period preceding his appointment to the Supreme Court amply prepared him for decision making in the cases relating to neutrality that came before him.

Negotiating on an international level required not only that Marshall fully understand the many problems that the United States encountered as a neutral but also the reasons behind the policy. Marshall's legal mind required him to master the law supporting the policy. Self-interest dictated the need for the United States to remain aloof from the wars enveloping Europe. Before and during the American Revolution, England, France, and Spain had used the colonies in North America as pawns in their larger struggle for power. The European nations retained this attitude after 1783. France's alliance with the United States during the Revolutionary War, extremely beneficial (if not decisive) to the cause of independence, was prompted and pursued by France to redress her defeat in the French and Indian War, resulting in the loss of all her possessions in the New World except the French West Indies. France hoped to capitalize on American gratitude and, more specifically, on the obligations contained in the Franco-American Treaty of Alliance of 1778.

The United States, attempting to become an independent commercial nation, adopted the relatively undeveloped concept in international law of neutrality.[28] Emmerich de Vattel had published *Les Droits des gens* in 1758, a treatise that presented the first formulation of a modern law of neutrality.[29] This work, "published shortly before the Revolution . . . became the authoritative textbook of the State Department and of the Federal Courts."[30]

Benjamin Franklin and John Adams were in Paris negotiating an end to the Revolution when the first major statement by a national government on neutrality was issued in 1780 by the Empress of Russia.[31] Franklin and Adams communicated during April, May, and June to the Continental Congress the progress of events concerning the principles of neutrality. Franklin expressed his hope that the law of nations would be changed to recognize the rights of neutrals. On October 5, 1780, the Continental Congress passed an act requesting that instructions based on the principles of neutrality be formulated by the Board of Admiralty. On November 27, the Congress adopted the following instructions which were issued to the commanders of United States armed vessels:

> 1. You shall permit all neutral vessels freely to navigate on the high seas or coasts of America, except such as are employed in carrying contraband goods or soldiers to the enemies of these United States.
> 2. You shall not seize or capture any effects belonging to the subjects of belligerent powers on board neutral vessels, excepting contraband goods.
> 3. The term contraband shall be confined to those articles which are expressly declared to be such in the treaty of amity and commerce, of the 6th of February, 1778, between these United States and his Most Christian Majesty, namely arms, great guns, bombs with their fuses and other things belonging to them, cannon ball, gun powder, match, pikes, swords, lances, spears, halberts, mortars, petards, grenadoes, saltpetre, muskets, musket ball, bucklers, helmets, breastplates, coats of mail, and the like kind of arms proper for arming soldiers, musket rests, belts, horses with their furniture, and all other warlike instruments whatever.[32]

The instructions paralleled Articles I, II, and III of the "fundamental rules" pronounced by the Empress Catherine. The article on blockade[33] was not included, but it expressed the position the United States would take on the subject of so-called paper blockades.

Washington, aware of the importance of neutrality to American commerce and national survival, issued the Proclamation of Neutrality in 1793. To guide the government on this uncharted course, the cabinet formulated rules of neutrality. These rules were drawn up by the Attorney General and circulated on August 4, 1793, by the Secretary of the Treasury to officers in charge of maritime ports. The rules, defining the rights and duties of neutrals, were formulated on "principles of international law . . .crystallized by a study of European study and practice."[34]

The rules were accompanied by instructions to the customs collector on handling violations. Arming and equipping ships for war in United States ports by any belligerent was declared illegal. Treaty obligations to the contrary were specifically excepted. Congress provided the legislation by which violators could be prosecuted when it passed the Neutrality Acts of June 5, 1794. Charles Fenwick describes the significance of the legislation:

> [It] set a standard of neutral conduct that was destined to have a marked effect upon the development of the international law of neutral duty. The act prohibited, within the territory or jurisdiction of the United States, the acceptance and exercise of a commission to serve a foreign prince or state, the enlistment or hiring to enlist in the service of a belligerent, the hiring to enlist abroad, the fitting out and arming within the ports of the United States of vessels intended to be used in the service of a foreign state against another foreign state with which the United States was at peace.[35]

## MARSHALL'S WRITINGS

### Instructions to the Commission

The mission was undertaken as an attempt to establish the neutral policy of the United States as the primary sources reveal. Marshall's appreciation for the legal position of the United States as a neutral was the controlling factor in his negotiations in France. The instructions issued to the three envoys contained the injunction that the principles of neutrality, "founded on the law of nations," were to inform the negotiations.[36] Ambitiously anticipating that every area of contention between France and the United States would become a subject for negotiation, the instructions provided a complete statement of the law of neutrality as the United States wished it applied to France. Accompanying the instructions were various documents including pertinent correspondence and reports. Pickering's instructions to Pinckney issued January 16, 1797, were included.[37] Significantly, the Pinckney instructions would add depth to Marshall's understanding. Marshall's study of the problems with France included the entire range of diplomatic issues and the international law related to those issues.

The envoys were instructed on the details of the complaints against France for violation of neutral rights (including the depredations on United

States commerce and the need for compensation to United States merchants for their losses), the offending French decrees (which authorized captures and confiscations of American vessels and of enemy property within neutral vessels), and the extended detention of American ships in French ports. The envoys were instructed, however, that they were not to make the settlement of the claims against France for maritime violations a condition precedent to negotiating a new treaty.

The envoys were to negotiate for changes in the commercial treaty with France on the two major points of contention, the definition of contraband and the seizure of enemy goods aboard neutral ships. They were authorized to extend the definition of contraband to correspond with the definition of Article XVIII of the Jay Treaty, i.e., to include ship timber, tar, sails, hemp and cordage. Contraband under Article XXIV of the 1778 treaty was narrowly restricted.[38] They were also authorized to change the provision that "*free ships make free goods*" contained in Article XXIII of the 1778 treaty to correspond to the provision in Article XVII of the Jay Treaty, which provided that all enemy property aboard a neutral ship was subject to confiscation.[39]

To prevent the seizure of ships not carrying the documentation required by the French, the envoys were instructed to agree specifically what documents were to be required of neutral vessels. In reliance on the principles of neutrality, they should insist that all blockades be actual, i.e. accept no mere declaration of blockades. They should also explicitly stipulate that a neutral vessel could enter without fear of detention or confiscation the port of an enemy. The envoys could relinquish France's guarantee of the liberty, sovereignty, and independence of the United States, and should seek to extricate the United States from the obligations under Article XI of the Treaty of Alliance to guaranty French possessions in America. The Rule of 1756, by which England "claimed a right and practiced upon it, to prohibit neutral nations carrying on a commerce with her enemies which had not been allowed in time of peace," should be excluded from all agreements with France.[40] Public ships of belligerents should have equal rights to United States ports on the principle of hospitality. French prizes were not to be sold in the United States by French consuls. Consular decisions were not to be enforced by the United States, but "by the laws of their proper country."[41] Privateers were not to be fitted out in neutral ports. Belligerent vessels were to be given twenty-four hours to clear port to avoid hostile movements within the jurisdiction of the United States. The parties should agree on the extent of territorial jurisdiction of the coast. Treaties should be limited in duration to ten or twenty years.

In addition to dealing with specific articles in the 1778 treaties that might need to be interpreted or changed, the envoys were to be guided by general considerations: (1) No blame or censure should be directly or indirectly imputed to the United States, (2) No aid should be stipulated in favour of France during the present war, (3) No engagement should be made inconsistent with the obligations of any prior treaty, (4) No restraint on the lawful commerce of the United States with any other nation should be admitted, and (5)

No stipulation allowing special privileges to French citizens or special tribunals should be established within the United States which might infringe upon the complete sovereignty and independence of United States.[42]

### Journal Entries: October 4, 1797—April 11,1798

With these instructions, Marshall and Pinckney arrived in Paris on September 27, 1797, and awaited the arrival of Gerry on October 4 before pressing their business. Constantly rebuffed in their application to be formally accepted, within two weeks, the envoys were informally entreated to

> give satisfaction to the honor of France wounded by the speech of the president, . . . to pay the debts due by contract from France to [United States] citizens . . . to pay for the spoliations committed on [United States] commerce for which France should be adjudged liable by commissioners to be appointed as in the British treaty . . . [to] make a considerable loan to an extent not defind [*sic*] . . . [and to] pay a considerable sum . . .for the private use of the Directoire & minister under the form of satisfying claims which did not in fact exist.[43]

Marshall's response to the steady demands was a clear-sighted assessment of a neutral's duty under such pressure:

> I told [Mr. Hottinguer] that . . . no nation estimated [France's] power more highly than America or wished more to be on amicable terms with her but that our object was still dearer to us than the friendship of France which was our national independence. that America had taken a neutral station. She had a right to take it. No nation had a right to force us out of it. That to lend a sum of money to a belligerent power abounding in every thing requisite for war but money was to relinquish our neutrality & take part in the war, to lend this money under the lash & coercion of France was to relinquish the government of ourselves & to submit to a foreign government imposed upon us by force.[44]

During the course of the informal meetings, Gerry showed a willingness to deal informally with the French, and he began to see Talleyrand secretly. By early February, the envoys were unable to agree among themselves on a common negotiating stance. Pinckney wrote to his brother late in the month, "Every art is used by Talleyrand and the French Americans here to divide the Envoys, and if possible to detach Mr. Gerry from his colleagues."[45] On February 18, 1798, the irrecoverable "breach" between the three envoys was exposed when Gerry refused to sign the letter of remonstrance penned by Marshall protesting the recently issued Decree confiscating all neutral vessels carrying British articles.[46] Marshall indicated that the split with Gerry was a matter of both substance and strategy:

> When this secret business first commenced I thought it my duty to tell Mr. Gerry that I was firmly convinced of the determination of this Government not to leave us our independence but to force us into the situation of her other allies: that all negotiation on their part would have that object in view and that a reconciliation on other terms was unattainable, . . . I was therefore decidedly of opinion that the object . . . was only to amuse us still longer and to prevent our taking those measures which would produce unequivocal explanations on the part of France.[47]

The overtures made by the French for a loan to be used "after the war" revealed the tenacity with which Marshall clung to his interpretation of neutrality. Late in the month of February, Marshall reported on a two-hour conference held by the envoys during which Gerry stressed the importance of making a loan to be used "after the war." Marshall doubted the request was serious and reiterated his conviction that "a loan under the actual circumstances of our Country would amount to a surrender of our national independence." Gerry "contended that the liberty and independence of our country had nothing to do with the question," and blamed Marshall for an unwarranted suspicion.[48]

On March 2, the envoys met with Talleyrand, and the subject of a loan to be used "after the war" was discussed. Marshall told him personally that "neutrality in the present war was of the last importance to the United States and they had resolved faithfully to maintain it." Talleyrand answered the objection that a loan would "draw" the United States out of its neutrality by suggesting "various means of avoiding this, first the secrecy of France which might be relied upon; and secondly means of disguising the loan might be devised which would effectually prevent its being considered as an aid during the present war." Marshall responded that the envoys "could do nothing in secret which if known would justly arrange them among the belligerent powers. That . . . to furnish money was in fact to make war. . . ."[49]

Talleyrand met with the three envoys again on March 6. After much discussion, they merely restated their respective positions but Marshall and Gerry indicated their willingness to return to the United States for instructions as to a loan to be used "after the war."[50] In resuming his position, Talleyrand insisted that "there was a difference . . . between a loan payable immediately, and a loan payable in future, and he still insisted there was no difference between a loan payable in future, and a credit for the money which might be due our citizens."[51] He had argued that the willingness of the United States to pay United States citizens for illegally obtained prize retained by the French was the same as making a loan to be paid in the future, but the American envoys disagreed and maintained that to recognize credit for funds illegally taken by France did not equate with the positive act of advancing money.[52]

By the date of the last entry in Marshall's journal on April 11, 1798, negotiations had broken down. Talleyrand hesitated to order Marshall and Pinckney to leave, and Marshall was loathe to demand his passport to leave. On April 13, Talleyrand issued passports to Marshall and Pinckney. Gerry, although he had intermittently protested against negotiating alone, stayed in Paris until late July, hoping to reach an accommodation. Pinckney, on doctors' orders, took his daughter to the south of France for her health. Marshall returned to the United States alone to a hero's welcome. During his absence, his wife had given birth to a son. At the time of his return, she was grieving over the recent death of her father.[53]

Marshall arrived in the United States with an increased knowledge in maritime and international law gained during six months of frustrated attempts to negotiate. Approximately four years before, Marshall had answered a client's inquiry about maritime salvage by admitting, "I am but little versd in marine law as I never practisd in the courts of admiralty & never turned my attention to the subject. Of consequence my opinion on the case you state is not much to be relied on."[54] The experience in Paris was invaluable to him as he would soon begin drafting final appellate decisions in cases involving maritime and international law, as well as reviewing maritime disputes at the Circuit Court level. During the mission to France, he had turned his attention to and had begun to master the subject in order to comprehend the problems faced by an emerging country asserting neutrality during maritime war.

## Letters from Paris

The letters which Marshall wrote while in Paris to Timothy Pickering, George Washington, and Charles Lee contained less-guarded reflections and comments on the mission to France. The letters to Pickering and Lee were in cipher. Marshall also wrote to Fulwar Skipwith, United States Consul General in Paris, on official matters arising from violations of the United States' neutrality. His significant comments are restricted to three recurring topics: the insults to neutrality witnessed in Europe, conditions in war-torn Europe, and the policy of the French government towards the United States and the commissioners.

Shortly after arriving in Paris, Marshall complained in a letter to Charles Lee about the delay in opening negotiations, and noted that "[i]n the meantime, our vessels are every day condemned and the money will soon be every day passing into the hands of the captors."[55] On October 24, Marshall wrote to Washington that "the captures of our vessels seem to be only limited by the ability to capture. That ability increasing as the government has let out to hardy adventurers the national frigates."[56]

Marshall wrote to Pickering in November about the American sailors who "belonging to the captured vessels . . . are thrown on shore without adequate support & without the means of returning" home. He theorized that the conditions of want and the promise of profit effectively impressed the men into service as sea rovers. He concluded that they "will be lost perhaps forever, but certainly, during the present war to their country."[57] Marshall addressed the fate of the sailors in correspondence with Fulwar Skipwith on December 20, 1797:

> The situation of our Sailors demands the immediate attention of our Government. We consider it as indispensably necessary to provide the means of their return to our Country. You will therefore please to inform the different Consuls that wherever opportunities of sending our Sailors home shall occur such opportunities shall be seized, & the necessary advances, not exceeding _______ per man, be made, for which the drafts of the Consul on the Ministers of the United States will be paid.[58]

In January, Marshall advised Skipwith to pay the requested sum for the release of sailors imprisoned at Brest, but to be certain that the "intervention of the United States be only usd" for those returning to the United States, the intention of the government being to take "all proper measures . . . to restore our fellow citizens to their friends their families & their liberty."[59]

Marshall delivered his most scathing remarks about the French government in a letter to Pickering in late October. "That she is not and never will be a republick is a truth which I scarcely dare whisper even to myself. It is in America and America only that human liberty has found an asylum."[60]

He described the fate of Americans' civil rights in France. Jesse Putnam, a Boston merchant in France as an agent to collect claims against the French government, was summarily arrested "without any examination of the case or regard to forms usual between debtor and creditor" and "committed to jail."[61] A New Yorker, James Murray, who was in Paris to collect for supplies sold to the government, although protected by a passport, was thrown "without any assignment of cause . . . into the common jail of felons" becoming "covered with filth & lice," and then sent under guard out of France. His brother, George W. Murray, a resident of Paris, was subsequently jailed.[62]

Perhaps prompted by the requests for money made of the envoys, Marshall spoke of the corruption in the French government. He expressed his fear to Charles Lee that the owners of the privateers were working against the mission by bribing officials,

> Some of the owners of privateers have been in Paris since our arrival and I think it not improbable that their object has been to exert their influence which unfortunately is very considerable to prevent any accommodation which may rescue from them the

> specie they have not yet received. I greatly fear they will succeed. It is said that Merlin when Minister of Justice received four thousand Louis from the owners of privateers for the direction concerning the *role d'equipage*. . . . I am persuaded that the courts . . . are political.[63]

To Washington, he confided his opinion that the government was "radically hostile" to the United States and his belief that "no consideration [would] be sufficiently powerful to check the extremities to which the temper of this government will carry it, but an apprehension that we may be thrown into the arms of Britain."[64]

In March, he described France as a "nation already tired of the war & groaning under the pressure of an enormous taxation." He wrote, "notwithstanding the enormous contributions made by foreign nations, France is overwhelmed with taxes . . .Real property pays in taxes nearly a third of its produce & is greatly reduced in price."[65]

Marshall thought the corrupt government's "difficulty in procuring funds" prevented more extensive conquests, noting, "It is the common opinion that shoud the elections in any respect disappoint the wishes of the Directory it will be on the side of Jacobinism. The existing government appears to me to need only money to enable it to effect all its objects."[66]

Marshall's comments about the violations of the rights of neutrals and the corrupt practices of the French government presented an unfavorable assessment of France. His letters also revealed that he recognized early that the mission would fail. This assessment remained unchanged as his irritation increased. After the first meeting with Talleyrand on October 8, Marshall wrote to Pickering,

> The personal demeanor of the Minister was polite and easy. We have not since heard from him in any manner whatever. It will appear strange to you as it does to us that this delay should be experienced. . . . We have some reason to believe that the effort of the government here be to break off or indeed prevent the commencement of negotiation . . . and thus the system of dividing us is to be kept up.[67]

Soon after this communication, Talleyrand requested money through the informal emissaries. On December 14, 1797, Marshall expressed to Pickering his belief that "if we were to remain here for six months longer, without we were to stipulate the payment of money, and a great deal of it, . . . we should not be able to effectuate the objects of our mission, . . . unless the projected attempt on England was to fail, or a total change takes place in the . . . this government."[68]

Over two months later, writing to Washington, Marshall expressed similar concerns:

> It was some little time past expected that, convinced of the unpracticability of effecting the objects of their mission, our ministers were about to demand their passports & to return to the United States. . . . The report has been that so soon as it shall be known that they will not add a loan to the mass of american property already in the hands of the government, they will be ordered out of France & a nominal as well as actual war will be commenced against the United States. My opinion has always been that this depends on the state of war with England.[69]

Marshall felt a deep sense of frustration and increasing irritation in the progress of the negotiations. On November 27, he wrote to his wife, "I now apprehend that it will not be in my power to reach America til April or May--but on this subject all is yet uncertain. . . . Oh God how much time & how much happiness have I thrown away."[70]

This note of despair, however, was only once recorded in his formal correspondence. "I have cursed a thousand times the moment when a sense of duty inducd me to undertake this painful embassy, but I must now make the best of it. I repeat my request that you will keep to yourself the contents of this letter except so far as to let it be known that we wait the orders of this or our government."[71]

### Memoranda to Talleyrand

Although the American envoys were never officially acknowledged by the French government, they met with Talleyrand informally at various times. They agreed to draft a memorial to be sent through him to the government, stating the United States position on the issues dividing the two countries.

Marshall spent two months drafting the document, submitting it to both Gerry and Pinckney for approval. It was submitted to Talleyrand on January 17, 1798. Marshall divided the memorial into two sections. In the first, he presented arguments to justify the United States' foreign policy. Specifically, he tried to reconcile the Jay Treaty with the Treaty of 1778. In the second part, he detailed the grievances of the United States against France. Marshall presented logical, forceful, and persuasive arguments to support his positions. He defined a treaty as a contract, and this definition formed the legal basis for his arguments. The editors of the Marshall Papers concluded that the document proved "that Marshall was, as John Adams observed 'learned in the law of nations'"[72] and noted that the document was studied by the second group of ministers to France as "the strongest statement on American rights and obligations toward France."[73]

To justify the United States position as a neutral, Marshall explained that the country, faced with a war "waged . . . with unparalleled fury," had considered its own interests as a trading nation, had examined its treaties and others, and had determined that it had a duty to remain neutral and aloof from the European wars. The government, once having taken this course, began the more difficult task of observing neutrality. Believing that "a fraudulent neutrality is no neutrality at all, and that the nation, which would be admitted to its privileges, must perform the duties it enjoins,"[74] the United States resolved to treat all nations as equal independent sovereigns.

Marshall found two sources for rules of conduct governing international behaviour, in treaties and in the law of nations. The law of nations, Marshall wrote, "forms, independent of compact, a rule of action by which the Sovereignties of the civilized world consent to be governed. It prescribes what one nation may do without giving just cause of war, and what of consequence another may and ought to permit without being considered as having sacrificed its honor, its dignity or its independence."[75]

Using this definition as a basis for his discussion of the Jay Treaty and the topics on which the debate over the treaty centered, Marshall asked, "What then is the doctrine of the law of nations, on this subject? Do neutral bottoms of right and independant of particular compact protect hostile goods?"[76] The status of enemy goods in neutral bottoms under the Jay Treaty, Marshall noted, was the same as the rule of the law of nations. "It is a general rule, that war gives to a belligerent power a right to seize and confiscate the goods of his enemy. . . . Thus it is admitted that an armed vessel may stop & search at sea a neutral bottom & may take out goods, which are contraband of war, without giving cause of offence, or being supposed in any degree to infringe neutral rights."[77]

An exception to this general rule, the exception incorporated as the ideal in the fundamental rules of neutrality advanced in 1780 by Empress Catherine,[78] and noticed by Marshall, had been written into the Treaty of Commerce between France and the United States in February of 1778: "[I]t stipulated in substance, that neither party should take out of the vessel of the other the goods of its enemy, but that the Character of the bottom should be imparted to its Cargo."[79]

Marshall noted that the Jay Treaty, which was silent on the subject, left the parties where they were, i.e. governed by the law of nations. Marshall contended that there was "no solid ground for maintaining, that the general law of nations ha[d] been at all varied by the armed neutrality."[80]

In this way, Marshall analyzed the position of the United States as to France and England and the effect of bottoms on cargo (i.e., he stated the law in relation to each). The United States was bound by treaty to respect the principle that neutral bottoms make neutral goods in dealing with France. The general rule of the law of nations controlled its relations with England, as no treaty provision applied. Marshall argued that the two treaty obligations were separate and distinct.

> It results from the very nature of a contract, which affects the rights of the parties, but not of others, and from the admission of a general rule of action binding independent of compact, which may be changed by consent, but is only changed so far as that consent is actually given, that a treaty between any two nations must leave to all others those rights, which the law of nations acknowledges, & must leave each of the contracting parties subject to the operation of such rights.[81]

Marshall informed Talleyrand that the United States desired to have the principle, neutral bottoms make neutral goods, established "universally." The ministers negotiating with Great Britain had tried to have the principle included in the Jay Treaty, but they could not obtain Britain's consent. Marshall contended that the United States would use "all proper means" to establish the principle but would not use force, and was not obligated by its treaty with France to honor the principle in its dealings with other nations. Marshall applied the consent requirement in contract law to treaties.

Consent formed the basis for the definition of contraband in each treaty obligation. Under the treaty of 1778, contraband excluded naval stores and lumber for shipbuilding. Citing Vattel, Book 7, § 112, Marshall noted that the accepted list of contraband under the law of nations included "timber for ship building, and naval stores for the equipment of vessels."[82] The treaty of 1778 was an exception to the law of nations agreed upon by the parties to the treaty. Under the Jay Treaty, the list of contraband accorded that sanctioned by the law of nations. Marshall noted that America was dedicated to restricting the list of contraband by all proper means and negotiated its treaties accordingly. The United States was, however, bound by the negotiating process which rested on the consent of the parties.

Marshall did not address the contention that a preference for England resulted from the different treaty agreements. He was content to justify legally the existence of the two different treaties.[83]

Marshall presented the complaints of the United States against France in two categories, the first being the uncontroverted claims owed United States citizens that remained unsatisfied. These, he listed. They included claims for property seized under the French national convention of May 9, 1793; claims for compensation for long detention of vessels at Bourdeaux in 1793 and 1794; claims on notes and "other evidences of debt" against the colonial administrations in the West Indies; claims for inadequate compensation for cargoes seized for the public use; and contract claims against the government for goods supplied.[84] Marshall then elaborated on the second category of complaints, those claims "founded on captures and confiscations, the illegality of which ha[d] not yet been admitted."

Marshall complained that the French had committed depredations on United States commerce pursuant to the May 1793 decree authorizing search and seizure of neutral vessels "loaded in whole or in part, either with provisions for neutrals & destined for enemy ports, or with merchandize belonging to enemies."[85] Under this decree, United States cargoes and vessels were confiscated as prize violating both the law of nations and the treaty agreements between France and the United States.

The Decree of March 2, 1797, was analyzed extensively. It purported to be a modification of the 1778 treaty which would give to France the same rights enjoyed by England under the Jay Treaty. Marshall showed that the rules 1, 2, and 3 adopted in the Decree to approximate the provisions of Articles XVII, XVIII, and XXI of the Jay Treaty were in fact broader.

The provisions relating to confiscation of enemy goods were contained in rule 1 and Article XVII. The French rule authorized confiscation of all "merchandise not sufficiently proved to be neutral." The Jay Treaty required that when a vessel was stopped "on just suspicion," if any property of an enemy should be found on board, ". . . that part only which belongs to the enemy shall be made prize." Marshall argued that the burden of proof shifted from the captor to the captured, who must prove the nature of the goods under the French rule. Under the Jay Treaty, the captor must "show the justice of the suspicion" and prove the nature of the goods.[86]

A comparison of the lists of contraband under the French rule 2 and Article XVIII revealed that the Decree enlarged the list by adding articles that "indirectly" served to arm or equip a vessel.[87]

Under rule 3, France purported to claim the rights enjoyed by the English under Article XXI. The United States and England agreed not to do acts of violence or hostility to each other and provided that a citizen of either country acting under a "foreign commission or letters of marque for arming a vessel to act as a privateer" could be treated and punished as a pirate. The French rule provided that "every individual known to be an american, who shall hold a commission given by the enemies of France, as well as every seaman of that nation making a part of the crew of enemy ships, shall by that act be declared a pirate and treated as such, without being allowed in any case to alledge that he was forced to do it by violence menaces or otherwise."[88] The French rule not only extended the definition of a pirate but also stripped the suspect of his civil rights.

Marshall found that rule 4 of the decree was "in its operation, the most extensive & the most seriously destructive."[89] This rule was a reinterpretation of the requirements under the 1778 treaty for proving the nature of the goods on vessels subject to confiscation. The new rule provided that a list of crew members, other papers, and a *role d'equipage* had to be produced. The countries had always accepted a passport as sufficient proof and Marshall argued that the correct interpretation of the treaty was the one under which the parties had been operating. According to Marshall, the treaty required a commander of a merchant ship to exhibit to ships of war and privateers only a passport to which an oath of the ship's cargo was appended. Marshall argued further that the long-continued practice under this interpretation of the treaty served to prove the substance of the requirement. The "new construction on a long, existing contract" worked extreme hardship which was not authorized or warranted.[90]

Marshall closed the memorial with the observation that French policy had caused "the most extensive and universal devastation of the American commerce," that "direct commerce between the two nations [was] almost annihilated & that the property of American citizens had been taken to a much larger amount than would have been possible in a state of actual war."[91]

The envoys offered the document as "an additional effort . . . to cultivate and restore . . . harmony between the two republics." Beveridge claimed that the statement made by Marshall was "one of the ablest state papers ever produced by American diplomacy."[92] Marshall mastered the details of the subject before him in lawyerly fashion. He applied the law to the facts. He had turned his attention to the subject, and would do so again.

Talleyrand responded on March 18, 1798, documenting France's grievances. Marshall worked eight days to answer the complaints enumerated by Talleyrand. He divided the complaints into three categories "1. The inexecution of their treaties with France. 2dly. The treaty of amity, commerce & navigation formed with Great Britain. 3dly. The conduct of their Government since that treaty."[93] Talleyrand complained that the United States violated treaty obligations on four counts: (1) Since 1793, United States courts had ruled on the validity of prizes brought into United States ports by French cruisers; (2) United States ports were open to the ships of France's enemy and their captures of French property; (3) United States courts ordered the arrest of *le Cassius* and the ship's captain; and (4) the United States refused to execute the consular convention of 1788. Quoting from the correspondence of Secretaries of State Thomas Jefferson and Edmund Randolph, Marshall minutely set forth the neutral position of the United States since 1793 in response to the assertions of French Ministers Genêt, Adet, and Fauchet. Marshall noted that the United States position was based on the principle of territorial integrity and national independence.

Responding to Tallyrand's charges regarding violations by the United States of the treaty with France, Marshall noted that Talleyrand "had not been pleased to state a case" in which the American courts exercised jurisdication over French prizes. To prove there were none, he referred to letters written by Jefferson and Randolph specifically denying any such authority or exercise.[94]

Marshall answered Talleyrand's specific complaint that the United States had violated the treaty obligation under Article XVII by which French ships with prizes were to be guaranteed access to United States ports, and the enemies of France (with any prizes) were to be kept out unless forced in by weather, in which case they were to be turned away as soon as possible. Marshall explained that the United States by "construction supposed to be just" had required the enemy war ships to leave, but had allowed the prizes to remain in safety. Marshall further noted that this construction of the treaty had determined United States actions since 1793, during which time France had acquiesced in the practice and had not insisted on a literal construction of the treaty provisions.[95]

Talleyrand had also protested the arrest of *le Cassius*, a.k.a. *les Jumeaux*, and the captain commandant. The ship, under the name of *les Jumeaux*, Marshall explained, was fitted out in Philadelphia in defiance of United States law. Before she could be apprehended she escaped, although the agent who fitted her out was tried, convicted, and imprisoned. The ship sailed to Santo Domingo, where it was commissioned by the French government as *le Cassius*, and when it sailed back to Philadelphia, the ship and captain were arrested as prize in the District Court. The Supreme Court issued a writ of prohibition to the lower court, on the basis that French "vessels of war and their officers, are not liable to process of our courts."[96] The ship was then attached in a suit instituted by creditors alleging it was a ship of war intending to make war on neutral nations. Marshall assured Talleyrand that the United States Attorney entered the case to defeat its prosecution, and the court dismissed the suit in 1796 on the basis of jurisdiction. Marshall asked whether a United States vessel would have fared so well in the French courts.[97]

The French complained that the United States had not executed its duties under the November 14, 1788, Consular Convention. They contended that United States judges were obligated to order arrests of persons declared to be deserters by consular judgments. Reviewing the language of the convention, Marshall found no agreement to execute consular judgments. Such a provision would "erect in a foreign country complete courts of justice" and be contrary to principles of independence.[98] United States judges were required to issue mandates for arrests of persons charged as deserters. The French complained that the judges demanded the original roll of the crew as evidence in the proceedings determining whether the mandate should be issued. Marshall concluded that the law required that the original be produced.

The answers to Talleyrand's complaints were cast in an argumentative tone. The expositions on many of the issues were thorough and logical. At times, Marshall seemed to be trying merely to score points on his adversary. His pique was transparent in answering the complaints about the Consular Convention. "The undersigned regret, citizen minister, that your researches concerning the United States have not extended to their Courts. You would have perceived & admired their purity. You would have perceived that America may repose herself securely on the integrity of her Judges; & your justice would have spared the insinuations concerning them, which have closed this part of your letter.[99]

Marshall's response to Talleyrand's comments on the Jay Treaty was basically argumentative, i.e."you say . . . by whom said?" The points of disagreement on substance had been explored in the January 17 document, and Marshall blamed Talleyrand for failure to state "any objection drawn from the compact itself."[100] He restated his earlier arguments that the treaty did not change the neutral position of the United States toward France.

Marshall addressed three specific complaints by Talleyrand regarding United States conduct after the Jay Treaty was signed. "lst. The refusal to permit in the ports of the United States the sale of prizes made by french cruisers."[101] Marshall admitted the truth of the matter and challenged Talleyrand to prove that this constituted a violation of the principles of neutrality or of prior treaty agreements. He argued that it was neither, noting that the 1778 treaty provisions merely required free access to the ports, and that a violation of neutrality required "a showing of partiality for one of the belligerent powers."[102]

"2dly. The invectives and calumnies against the french government, its principles, & its officers, contained in certain journals and pamphlets published in the United States."[103] Marshall responded that "[t]he Genius of the Constitution & the opinions of the people of the United States cannot be overruled by those who administer the government." He expatiated on the liberty of the press:

> That this liberty is often carried to excess, that it has sometimes degenerated into licentiousness, is seen and lamented; but the remedy has not yet been discovered. Perhaps it is an evil inseparable from the good to which it is allied., perhaps it is a shoot which cannot be stripped from the stalk, without wounding vitally the plant from which it is torn. However desirable those measures may be, which might correct without enslaving the press, they have never yet been devised in America. No regulations exist which enable the government to suppress whatever calumnies or invectives any individual may chuse to offer to the public eye, or to punish such calumnies and invectives otherwise, than by a legal prosecution in courts, which are alike open to all who consider themselves as injured.[104]

"3dly. The speech of the President of the United States to Congress in may last."[105] Marshall defended Adams's speech of May 16, 1797, by again invoking the Constitution. He instructed the minister on the Constitutional requirement that the President inform Congress on the State of the Union, quoted from portions of the speech, and added his hope that France would view the speech in "its true light"—"not as a denunciation of the Directory," but as a "statement of an all important fact by one department of the American government to another."[106]

Marshall's statement to Talleyrand on January 17, 1798 was a reasoned analysis of the issues dividing the two countries. His response on April 3, 1798 to Talleyrand's complaints afforded him an opportunity to argue his case. Thwarted in all attempts to negotiate, Marshall, through these two written documents, may be said to have made his case. He stated it and he argued it.

Denied a courtroom, he merely approached the bench. He took away with him the whole case.

Had Marshall not experienced the mission to France, he would have been unprepared for the issues raised in the cases involving prize and neutrality. He had no experience in maritime trade or the life of the sea. Although he began practice in 1780, he admittedly had never practiced in the courts with maritime jurisdiction. Although he served during the Revolutionary War, his experience did not include participation in maritime exploits. Appointed deputy judge advocate, Marshall's legal experience during the war was limited to clerk duties and courts-martial proceedings. During an "inactive interval," he did visit his father who was in command of troops at Yorktown,[107] where possibly he learned something about maritime warfare.

Although he lived in Virginia, there is no indication that he participated in coastal life. Marshall's interests and experiences were bound to the land.[108] When he left for Paris, he planned, as a member of a land syndicate purchasing the Fairfax lands, to return through England to further the business. Convinced by Beaumarchais that such a return would be a diplomatic error, Marshall dropped the idea.[109] While in Paris, Marshall reported to Washington on agricultural conditions, "The whole earth appears to be in cultivation & the harvests of the present year appear to be as productive as the fields which yield them are extensive."[110] Marshall is reported to have carried seeds in his pockets throughout his life. As a member of the Virginia gentry, he never lost his attachment to the land or his interest in agriculture.

Against this background, Marshall's trip to Europe was an adventure which introduced him not only to a new area of the law of nations but also to the world of maritime war, from which much of that law developed. Marshall left Philadelphia on July 17, 1797, on the brig *Grace*, arriving in Amsterdam the night of August 29. During his trip, no "french, spanish or dutch ships" were encountered, but the ship was "boarded by some english frigates" and, "by some unaccountable account, all the ships papers were lost so that the vessel was lawful prize."[111]

After several days in Amsterdam, Marshall described the beseiged city:

> The mouth of the Texel is blockd up by a british fleet under Admiral Duncan who have for about a fortnight forbid the entrance of any vessel whatsoever. . . . In the mouth of the Texel lies a dutch fleet at least equal to the british which is said to have received orders to sail out, as soon as the wind is favorable, & to engage the enemy. . . . I askd the other day a very eminent merchant who politely gave me a ride round the city in his carriage how many french troops there were in Holland. He coud not tell me. I askd who was their general? He coud not tell. I askd some other questions to which he answerd

that he never meddled with politics.[112]

Marshall's most extensive report of personal observations on the war in Europe was written to Washington. "Until our arrival in Holland we saw only British & neutral vessels. This added to the blockade of the dutch fleet in the Texel, of the french fleet in Brest & of the spanish fleet in Cadiz manifests the entire dominion which one nation at present possesses over the seas."[113]

Marshall was in Amsterdam when Napoleon took over the French Directory on September 4. Napoleon established French hegemony over continental Europe the year after Marshall returned to the United States and the Napoleonic period (1799-1815) began. In addition to the panoramic view of warring Europe, Marshall had with him "more books than [he could] read during the passage."[114] Personal observation, study, and negotiation combined to prepare Marshall for decision making in maritime cases. The United States, as a neutral nation seeking an international trade, would continue to be exploited by the powers of Europe. To prosecute maritime wars during this period, belligerents commissioned private vessels with letters of marque and reprisal to prey on their enemies. Publicly owned vessels, although used, were expensive to build, maintain and keep. Privateers paid their way.[115] The issuance of letters of marque and reprisal as a means of conducting war was so important that the statesmen in Philadelphia in 1787 gave it constitutional status.[116]

In response to intense maritime warfare, the law of neutrality gained added importance during the late eighteenth and early nineteenth centuries. Neutral nations on commercial voyages were attacked by belligerents to cut off supplies to their enemies. The law of neutrality covered many issues brought before the prize courts. Appeals to the Supreme Court in prize cases proliferated during Jefferson's presidency and continued throughout the War of 1812 well into the 1820's.[117]

Marshall began his term on the Court when the Quasi-War with France had been resolved. The first case he decided when he became Chief Justice, *Silas Talbot v. Seeman* (1801),[118] grew out of that war and involved the French decree of 1798, issued while Marshall was in France, to which he had filed a remonstrance. Marshall noted only in passing that the decree was a violation of the law of nations, that "remonstrance [was] the proper course" to protest such violation, and that the United States, when remonstrance failed, took the step, sanctioned by the law of nations, of authorizing "limited hostilities." The facts of the case dictated that the decree be enforced. Marshall took judicial notice of the foreign decree, not requiring that it be proved as part of the judicial code of France.

The *Amelia*, owned by a citizen in neutral Hamburgh, was initially captured as prize by a French corvette under the Decree of January 18, 1798, and taken to St. Domingo where Captain Talbot, commanding the *USS Constitution*, re-took her, and libeled her in New York under a 1799 Congressional act passed to prosecute the undeclared war with France. The act allowed one-half of the value of the ship and cargo as prize to the crew.[119] Marshall ruled that the recapture was lawful, and that the captor was entitled to salvage.[120] The *Amelia* had on board a cargo from Calcutta. The Decree of 1798 made lawful prize of any ship carrying British goods. Marshall reasoned that she would have been condemned in a French court pursuant to the decree. The neutral owner upon payment of salvage for the service rendered by the *USS Constitution* was entitled to reclaim the ship.

Marshall's assumption that the French would enforce the Decree of 1798 was based not only on the recognition that the municipal law passed in pursuance of war superceded the law of nations but also on the fact that he had closely watched the process by which the decree was adopted. On January 8, 1798, the envoys had written to Pickering that the Directory had sent a message "to the Council of Five Hundred, urging the necessity of a Law to declare as good prize all Neutral Ships met at sea, whose cargoes, in part or in whole should consist, of Merchandizes or Commodities, the production of England, or of the English possessions, and that the Flag as they term it, may no longer cover the property."[121] The postscript added that the law passed unanimously and would "no doubt" be adopted "without opposition by the Council of Ancients." On February 7, the envoys wrote that the Council had passed the decree.

Marshall had then prepared a letter of remonstrance to Talleyrand protesting the decree. Because Gerry refused to sign it,[122] the letter was not sent, but forwarded to Pickering, signed by Marshall and Pinckney, and filed with the diplomatic dispatches. Marshall incorporated the substance of the remonstrance into the two statements signed by the three envoys that were sent to Talleyrand. The envoys protested that the decree would be detrimental to the "internal economy of nations, and derange that course of industry which they had a right to pursue and on which their prosperity depends." Noting that the object was to "cut off all direct intercourse between neutrals and Great Britain, or its possessions," they expressly mentioned that it violated Article XXIII of the 1778 Treaty of Amity and Commerce which provided that free ships make free goods.[123]

In the first term, Marshall also delivered the opinion in the case, *United States v. Schooner Peggy* (1801). The public ship *Trumbull* was commissioned by the President of the United States "to take any armed French vessel or vessels sailing under authority or pretence of authority from the French republic" either within territorial limits or on the high seas.[124] The *Trumbull* captured the schooner *Peggy* on April 23, 1800, libeled her in the District Court and was denied prize. The Circuit Court reversed, and on September 23, 1800, ordered the vessel forfeited to the use of the United States—one-half of the proceeds of the sale to go to the United States and one-half to the captors.

The Convention with France was signed in September of 1800, ratified on February 18, 1801, and proclaimed on December 21, 1801. It provided that captured property not "definitively condemned" should be mutually restored. Marshall held that the treaty provisions reached the *Peggy* and ordered her restored. He reasoned that she had not been "definitively condemned" as an appeal from the Circuit Court was pending when the Convention was signed. Marshall found that a controlling law, the treaty, had intervened to change the legal relationship of the parties. Acknowledging that the court should avoid giving retrospective effect to the treaty, Marshall reasoned that "in great national concerns where individual rights, acquired by war, are sacrificed for national purposes," the nation could take the vested rights of the citizens and perhaps owed compensation for the taking. Marshall, however, found that compensation was a political question, to be considered by the "government," not the Court.[125]

During his first term on the Bench, Marshall heard only these two cases arising from the Quasi-War with France. In these cases, his experience in diplomacy aided his judgment. The failure of the first mission to France had prompted the laws under which the cases arose. The success of the second mission to France controlled the outcome in the *Talbot* case. Marshall did not recuse in the cases because his private affairs were not directly related to the issues. The cases involved affairs of state in which Marshall had participated but Marshall, as a Federalist statesman, did not doubt that he could be neutral and objective in affairs of state. He recused in *Martin v. Hunter's Lessee* (1816)[126] because his private title to the Fairfax lands was in issue.

Marshall wrote the opinions in four other cases which involved Quasi-War disputes. Following the failure of the first mission, Congress passed acts of defensive warfare, providing for seizure of offending French vessels and awards of prize calculated to encourage capture.[127] A series of non-intercourse acts prohibited trade with France, and provided penalties of seizure and confiscation, as well as prize distribution between the captors and the informant. Marshall's decisions in the four cases brought to the Supreme Court under the non-intercourse provisions represented "a reaffirmation of traditional American views concerning the rights of neutrals."[128]

In *Maley v. Shattuck* (1806),[129] Jared Shattuck's vessel, the *Mercator*, was seized as prize of war on May 15, 1800, by William Maley, commanding the *Experiment*, a public armed vessel. Shattuck sought damages from Maley for the illegal taking. Maley contended that he thought the *Mercator* was a French vessel. Marshall noted the similarities of the two cases, *Murray v. The Charming Betsy* and *Maley v. Shattuck*. Jared Shattuck owned both vessels, which were taken as prizes of war under the non-intercourse act passed by Congress on February 9, 1799. Marshall, in the previous case, had found that Shattuck was a Danish burgher, a citizen of a neutral state, and he reaffirmed that ruling in *Maley*. The *Mercator*, being a neutral vessel, was not subject to confiscation as war prize; and Marshall assessed damages against Maley personally, noting that "The circumstances of suspicion arising in the case, were not sufficiently strong to justify the seizure which was made."[130]

In *Little v. Barreme* (1804),[131] Marshall also delivered the opinion. On December 2, 1799, the neutral brigantine *Flying Fish* was captured near the island of Hispaniola by the United States frigate *Boston*, commanded by Captain Little. The vessel was libeled as a United States vessel doing business with the enemy. The lower court had restored the ship and cargo to the neutral owner, but had not allowed damages for illegal capture, finding instead that there was probable cause. Marshall affirmed the decision.

In the case, *Sands v. Knox* (1806),[132] Thomas Knox, administrator of the estate of Raapzat Heyleger, a neutral Danish merchant, sued Joshua Sands, the customs collector for the port of New York, for detention of the vessel *Jennett*. The vessel, under the name of *Juno*, had sailed under bond with a cargo to the island of St. Croix in the West Indies, and to Port de Paix in St. Domingo, ports proscribed by the act. The owner of the *Juno* sold the vessel at St. Croix (then a Danish possession) to Raapzat Hyleger. Upon returning to the New York port, the vessel was seized by the customs collector for violation of the 1798 non-intercourse act. Marshall reasoned that "the law did not intend to affect the sale of vessels of the United States, or to impose any disability on the vessel after a bona fide sale and transfer to a foreigner."[133]

These cases arising from the Quasi-War illustrate that Marshall enforced international law with a due respect for the objective requirements of probable cause and intent. He construed the law to effect the rights of neutrals. He was aware, as evidenced in his arguments to Talleyrand, that search and seizure was a right to be exercised only on belligerent goods and vessels. By objectively allowing damages, he helped to police a practice subject to abuse. In this way, he continued to protest the violation of neutral rights.

Prize cases during the first two decades of Marshall's term came with great regularity, as the war on the Continent continued and the War of 1812 increased prize activity. As Secretary of State, Marshall gained an even greater appreciation for the power struggles of Europe and the laws that guided their affairs. In 1815, Henry Wheaton published *A Digest of the Law of Maritime Captures and Prizes*, in which he claimed that the law of prize was the "most important practical branch of the law of nations."[134]In describing his intention to quote jurists' opinions, he revealed the distinction in the field Marshall enjoyed:

> In the customary or *unwritten* law of nations, to borrow an analogous distinction from our municipal law, it is frequently of as much importance to give the very words of the legislator (for the elementary writer or the judge, who make law by their authority and precedents, must be so considered) as it is to transcribe the articles of a treaty or an ordinance, which, by the same analogy, form the *written* or statute law of nations. And who would presume to correct and amend the style of a Bynkershoek, a Pothier, a Scott, or a Marshall?[135]

Marshall's role in defining neutral rights and duties during this period was acknowledged in a series of letters on international law published from

1861 to 1863 in the *Times* in London, which were reprinted and published separately in 1863 as *Letters by Historicus.*[136] In the preface, the author discussed the sources in international law in the area of neutrality. He deplored the fact that "an adequate work on the Rights and Duties of Neutral Nations ha[d] yet to be written." England's proclaimed policy of neutrality during the Civil War in the United States prompted the discussion not only of the wisdom of the course, but also of the requirements of such a policy.

The author reviewed the slight accomplishments in the literature, mentioning the works of Kent and Wheaton. Kent's *Commentaries* he found "a perfect specimen of juridical exposition . . . too deficient in detail to supply the place of a practical treatise." He rated Wheaton's *The Elements of International Law* "next to that of Kent, the best general attempt which ha[d] yet been made at a discussion of the questions" of neutrality."[137] However, "of all the sources of authority on these subjects, the most valuable . . . are the decisions of the American Courts, . . . which for learning, impartiality, logic and good sense are unsurpassed in juridical annals."[138] "Historicus," discussing the task of finding the law of neutrality, described the problems that Marshall also confronted. In most questions of international law, the student must "make for himself his own textbook; to extract from scattered documents the records of historical precedents; to deduce from judicial decisions the principles of established law; and what is still more difficult, to distinquish in contradictory textwriters the doctrines which are founded on reason and law."[139]

The foreign policy of neutrality proclaimed by Washington in 1793 formed the basis of Marshall's political outlook in affairs of state. He went to France in an effort to disentangle the United States from the Treaty of Alliance of 1778 with instructions to assert the rights of neutrality and to negotiate with France as a neutral. Under the Convention of 1800, the United States attained the legal status of neutral vis-a-vis France. The United States' policy of neutrality toward all of Europe was prompted by the developing nation's desire to trade. It remained the dominant foreign policy throughout Marshall's tenure on the Court. The War of 1812 was fought partially because nations refused to accept the United States role as a neutral nation. Marshall's writings during the mission to France indicate that he was well prepared to write the decisions reflecting development in this area of international law.

## NOTES

1. Beveridge, *The Life of John Marshall*, vol. 2, p. 224.

2. Richard R. Beeman, *The Old Dominion and the New Nation, 1788-1801* (Lexington: University Press of Kentucky, 1972), pp. 137-51. Although Beeman interpreted this as a dilatory tactic, the argument is consistent with Marshall's understanding of the treaty making power.

3. *Ibid.*, p. 137.

4. Harry Ammon, *The Genêt Mission* (New York: W. W. Norton & Co., 1973), p. 146. Ammon reported that Genêt commissioned four privateers within a few days of his arrival, the *Republican*, the *Sans-Cullotte*, the *Anti George* and the *Citizen Genêt*. These privateers were fitted out and were "soon sending into Charleston English ships captured as prizes." *Ibid.*, at 44.

5. *Ibid.*, p. 170.

6. From the dispatches of Citizen Genêt and his successors, Pierre-Auguste Adet and Joseph Fauchet, Historian Henry Ammon concluded that it was French "determination to oust the Federalists which led the Directory into the Quasi-War." Ammon, *The Genêt Mission*, p. 170.

7. The Republicans thought that Marshall was a poor choice for the mission. Gerry accused him of being non-accommodating. Marshall records in his journal Gerry's telling him on March 6, 1798, "that he had heard nothing from me yet, which was accommodating." Journal entry of March 6, 1798. William C. Stinchcombe and Charles T. Cullen, eds., *The Papers of John Marshall: Correspondence and Papers, January 1796-December 1798* (Chapel Hill: The University of North Carolina Press, 1979), vol. 3, p. 223.

8. William C. Stinchcombe, *The XYZ Affair* (Westport, Conn.: Greenwood Press, 1980), p. 4.

9. Pickering substituted W, X, Y, and Z for the names of Nicholas Hubbard, Jean Hottinguer, Pierre Bellamy, and Lucien Hauteval appearing in the dispatches. As Hubbard was mentioned only twice, W was ignored. There was some confusion about W's identity. Caron de Beaumarchais who also met with the envoys was erroneously thought by some to be W. Stinchcombe, *The XYZ Affair*, pp. 3-11. See also Stinchcombe and Cullen, eds., *The Papers of John Marshall*, vol. 3, pp. 154-55, 168 n. 25, 191 n. 77, 314 n. 7.

10. From Timothy Pickering, July 15, 1797, Stinchcombe and Cullen, eds., *The Papers of John Marshall*, vol. 3, p. 118.

11. This refusal could be considered unnecessary under the instruction that the envoys refrain from trading accusations and merely terminate their differences without referring to the "merits" of their "respective complaints and pretensions." The guidelines, however, required that no blame or censure be imputed to the United States, but, in the effort not to "wound [France] or to excite resentment," the envoys were urged to accept the "principle of the British Treaty" as stated. See Letter to envoys from Timothy Pickering, July 15, 1797, Stinchcombe and Cullen, *Papers of John Marshall*, vol. 3, p. 117. Marshall held informal conversations with Caron de Beaumarchais, his client, who was also acting as an intermediary for Talleyrand. Although he told the other envoys about these conversations, he did not record Beaumarchais's name in the Journal. There is no evidence that the negotiations were influenced by these conversations. *Id.*, p. 155.

12. See instructions from Timothy Pickering, Secretary of State, July 15, 1797. "When the war was kindled between France and the powers of Europe . . . no duty required us to enter into the war, and our best interests

urged us to remain at peace, the Government determined to take a neutral station: which being taken, the duties of an impartial neutrality became indispensably binding." Stinchcombe and Cullen, eds., *The Papers of John Marshall*, vol. 3, p. 103.

13. Journal entry of October 30, 1797, Stinchcombe and Cullen, ed., *Papers of John Marshall*, vol. 3, p. 180.

14. *Ibid.*, pp. 182-83.

15. Journal entry of March 14, 1798, Stinchcombe and Cullen, ed., *The Papers of John Marshall*, vol. 3, p. 230.

16. *Ibid.*

17. *Virginia National Gazette, and General Advertiser*, August 24, 1978.

18. *Ibid.*

19. William C. Stinchcombe, "Talleyrand and the American Negotiators of 1797-1798," *Journal of American History* 62, no. 3 (December, 1975): 575-90.

20. William C. Stinchcombe, "The Diplomacy of the WXYZ Affair," *William and Mary Quarterly* 34, 3d ser. (1977): 590-617, at 590.

21. Randolph Greenfield Adams, *A History of the Foreign Policy of the United States* (New York: The Macmillan Company, 1924), p. 109.

22. The treaty, the Convention of Peace, Commerce, and Navigation Between the United States and France, was concluded in September of 1800 and ratifications were exchanged on July 31, 1801. See Miller, ed., *Treaties and other International Acts*, vol. 2, pp. 457-82. Robert H. Ferrell attributed the willingness of France to negotiate to the fact that the war had "taken a turn unfavorable to France." He also found that "in the making of peace the French used the Americans for their purposes in Europe." He explained that Napoleon hoped the treaty would bring the United States into a union of armed neutrality with neutrals on the Continent, and he noted that Napoleon used the treaty as political fodder by having it signed at festivities conducted at Joseph Bonaparte's country estate, Mortefontaine, and attended by all of the Bonapartes. See Robert H. Ferrell, *American Diplomacy, A History* (New York: W. W. Norton & Co., Inc., 1975), p. 92.

23. Beveridge, *The Life of John Marshall*, vol. 2, p. 522, n. 1, quoting the *Philadelphia Aurora*, March 4, 1800.

24. *Ibid.*, p. 524-25, n. 5. Quoting letters from Marshall to Hamilton, Jan 1, 1801, and from Rutledge to Hamilton, Jan. 10, 1801.

25. Jefferson to du Pont, April 25, 1802, Dumas Malone, ed., *Correspondence between Thomas Jefferson and Pierre Samuel du Pont de Nemours, 1798-1817* (New York: Houghton Mifflin Company, 1930), p. 48.

26. John Marshall to J. K. Paulding, April 4, 1835, Marshall Papers, Manuscript Division, Library of Congress, Washington, D.C.

27. Henry J. Ford, "Timothy Pickering," Samuel Flagg Bemis, ed., *The American Secretaries of State and Their Diplomacy* (New York: Alfred A. Knopf, 1927). Ford notes that the instructions are not in Pickering's

"style." "The internal evidence suggests that John Marshall's pen was employed upon them, in conformity with the common diplomatic practice of preventing misunderstanding by having the envoy draft his instructions." p. 217. Magruder also makes this observation.

28. Charles G. Fenwick described the acceptance of the concept of neutrality in the world of nations. As a concept, it replaced the just war theories which required a nation to take sides in controversies among fellow nations. He noted that the "feudal system precluded neutrality." Grotius in 1625 in *Law of War and of Peace* "recognize[d] that a nation might remain neutral," but the "influence of the moral law" prompted him to expect that a neutral, one "who in time of war [was] in a position between the contending parties," would study the issues and choose sides. The Swiss publicist Vattel significantly advanced the acceptance of the concept of neutrality in his treatise on the law of nations published in 1758. Commerce gave the impetus for the new concept. See Charles G. Fenwick, *American Neutrality: Trial and Failure* (New York: New York University Press; London: Oxford University Press, 1940), at pp. 6-12. See also Philip C. Jessup and Francis Deak, *Neutrality: Its History, Economics and Law, The Origins*, (New York: Columbia University Press, 1935), vol. 1.

29. Jessup and Deaks, *Neutrality: Its History, Economics and Law*, vol. 1, p. 4.

30. Fenwick, *American Neutrality*, p. 11. In 1775, Benjamin Franklin received three copies of Vattel's work from a Swiss publisher, Charles W. F. Dumas. Franklin thanked him and added that the book arrived at a time "where the circumstances of a rising state" necessitated frequent recourse to the law of nations. Nussbaum, *A Concise History of the Law of Nations*, quoted at p. 161.

31. The Americans were well aware of the emphasis in Europe concerning the rights of neutrals. On April 10, 1780, John Adams, in Paris to negotiate the terms of the peace of 1783, sent a copy of the declaration of Armed Neutrality issued by the Empress of Russia to the Continental Congress. The *envoy extraordinaire* from Russia, Prince Gallitzin, had presented a memorandum to the States-General explaining the Russian position. Adams considered the declaration "of too much importance to the United States of America and her allies to be omitted to be sent to Congress." John Adams to President of the Continental Congress, Carlton Savage, ed., *Policy of the United States Toward Maritime Commerce in War: 1776-1914* (Washington: Government Printing Office, 1934), vol. 1, p. 140. The Continental Congress passed a resolution June 12, 1783, regarding the rights of neutral nations.

32. *Ibid.*, pp. 149-50.

33. *Ibid.*, p. 142. For the Declaration of Her Majesty the Empress of Russia, made to the Courts of Versailles, Madrid, and London and mailed with correspondence from Adams to President Huntington, April 10, 1780, see *supra*, fn. 78.

34. Samuel Flagg Bemis, "Thomas Jefferson," *The American Secretaries of State and Their Diplomacy* (New York: Alfred A. Knopf, 1927), p. 81, n. 29. The rules are listed at pp. 296-98.

35. Fenwick, *American Neutrality*, pp. 116-17. The neutrality acts, which define the United States' duties as a neutral in international law, were extended in 1818 and are codified in 18 U.S.C. sections 963-67.

36. Secretary of State Pickering to the three envoys, July 15, 1797, Stinchcombe and Cullen, ed., *The Papers of John Marshall*, vol. 3, pp. 102-19.

37. Savage, ed., *Policy of the United States*, vol. 1, p. 310.

38. The definition of contraband in the 1778 treaty corresponds to the definition proclaimed in 1780 by the Empress of Russia and accepted by the Continental Congress the same year. The United States abandoned its preferred definition of contraband in the treaty with England who always insisted on a broader definition. France's complaint that the agreement worked a preference was justified, and the United States was ready to negotiate the issue.

39. Stinchcombe and Cullen, ed., *The Papers of John Marshall*, vol. 3, p. 106.

40. *Ibid.*, p. 107.

41. *Ibid.*, p. 116.

42. *Ibid.*, p. 117.

43. Journal entry of October 18-[19], 1797. Stinchcombe and Cullen, *The Papers of John Marshall*, vol. 3, pp. 164-65.

44. *Ibid.*, Journal entry of August 27, 1797, p. 173.

45. *Ibid.*, C. C. Pinckney to Thomas Pinckney, February 22, 1798, quoted at p. 197, n. 93.

46. *Ibid.*, p. 195, n. 88. The letter signed by Pinckney and Marshall was sent to Pickering via Rufus King, ambassador in England.

47. *Ibid.*, Journal entry of February 10, 1798, p. 199.

48. *Ibid.*, Journal entry of February 26, 1798, pp. 204-5.

49. *Ibid.*, Journal entry of March 2, 1798, pp. 217-18.

50. *Ibid.*, Journal entry of March 6, 1798, p. 228.

51. *Ibid.*, p. 226.

52. *Ibid.*, p. 228.

53. When Marshall returned, his wife, suffering from "chronic melancholia," was in Winchester, recuperating since the early summer in the home of John Marshall's brother. Mary W. (Polly) Marshall's father, Jaquelin Ambler died January 12, 1798, and her fourth child, John Marshall, was born January 23, 1798. Stinchcombe and Cullen, ed., *The Papers of John Marshall*, vol. 3, p. 468, n. 3, p. 487, n. 3. Marshall's return to an ailing and distraught wife is described in Frances Norton Mason, *My Dearest Polly: Letters of the Chief Justice to His Wife, 1779-1831* (Richmond: Garrett and Massie, 1961), pp. 113-23.

54. Marshall to Charles Simms, December 12, 1794, Cullen and

Johnson, ed., *The Papers of John Marshall*, vol. 2, p. 301.

55. *Ibid.*, Marshall to Charles Lee, October 12, 1797, p. 247.

56. *Ibid.*, Marshall to Washington, October 24, 1797, p. 401.

57. *Ibid.*, Marshall to Pickering, November 27, 1797, p. 303.

58. *Ibid.*, Marshall to Skipwith, December 20, 1797, p. 312.

59. *Ibid.*, Marshall to Skipwith, January 17, 1798, pp. 327-28.

60. *Ibid.*, Marshall to Pickering, October 25, 1798, p. 251.

61. *Ibid.*, Marshall to Charles Lee, November 3, 1797, p. 274; Marshall to Pickering, November 27, 1797, p. 301.

62. *Ibid.*, p. 302.

63. *Ibid.*, Marshall to Charles Lee, October 12, 1797, p. 247.

64. *Ibid.*, Marshall to Washington, October 24, 1797, p. 270.

65. *Ibid.*, Marshall to Washington, March 8, 1798, pp. 400, 402.

66. *Ibid.*, p. 401.

67. *Ibid.*, Marshall to Pickering, October 12, 1797, pp. 247, 250.

68. *Ibid.*, p. 317.

69. *Ibid.*, Marshall to Washington, March 8, 1798, p. 399.

70. *Ibid.*, Marshall to Mary Marshall, November 27, 1797, p. 229.

71. *Ibid.*, Marshall to Charles Lee, March 4, 1798, p. 397.

72. *Ibid.*, p. 330.

73. *Ibid.*, p. 331.

74. *Ibid.*, p. 335.

75. *Ibid.*, p. 338.

76. *Ibid.*, pp. 338-39.

77. *Ibid.*, p. 339. Marshall cited Vattel, Book 3, § 115, for the proposition that enemy goods on neutral ships are subject to seizure.

78. The Empress Catherine ordered "a considerable portion of her maritime forces [to be] put out to sea, with no other intention than to insure the observation of the most exact and the most strict neutrality." The five articles of neutrality contained in her declaration are:

> ARTICLE I. That all neutral vessels ought to navigate freely from one port to another, as well as upon the coasts of the powers now at war.
>
> ART. II. That the effects belonging to the subjects of the belligerent powers shall be free in neutral ships, excepting always contraband goods.
>
> ART. III. That her imperial majesty, in consequence of the limits above fixed, will adhere strictly to that which is stipulated by the tenth and eleventh articles of her treaty of commerce with Great Britain, concerning the manner in which she ought to conduct towards all belligerent. [These articles limited contraband to arms and munitions of war.]
>
> ART. IV. That as to what concerns a port blocked up, we ought not, in truth, to consider as such any but those which are found so well shut up by a fixed and sufficient number of vessels

belonging to the power which attacks it that one can not attempt to enter into such port without evident danger.

ART. V. That these principles above laid down ought to serve as a rule in all proceedings, whenever there is a question concerning the legality of prizes.

Enclosure in letter of John Adams to Confederation President Huntington, April 10, 1780, Savage, ed., *Policy of the United States Toward Maritime Commerce in War: 1776-1914*, Document 6, p. 142.

79. Stinchcombe and Cullen, ed., *The Papers of John Marshall*. vol. 3, p. 338.

80. *Ibid.*, p. 341.

81. *Ibid.*, p. 342.

82. *Ibid.*, p. 352.

83. The editors of *The Marshall Papers* remark that Marshall's reasoning is unrealistic, although logical, as the "major issue between France and the United States was how the Jay Treaty had changed relations between the United States and France." *Ibid.*, vol. 3, p. 347, n. 1. The major issue, however, to Marshall was the depredation inflicted by the French on United States' citizens and property, and he was determined to assert the rights of the United States to treat as an independent nation.

84. *Ibid.*, p. 365.

85. *Ibid.*, p. 345.

86. *Ibid.*, pp. 369-70.

87. *Ibid.*, p. 370.

88. *Ibid.*, pp. 371-72.

89. *Ibid.*, p.372.

90. *Ibid.*, pp. 373-79.

91. *Ibid.*, p. 379.

92. Beveridge, *The Life of John Marshall*, vol. 2, p. 297. The editors of *The Marshall Papers* note that Beveridge's claim was probably an exaggeration. Stinchcombe and Cullen, ed., *The Papers of John Marshall*, vol. 3, p. 331.

93. *Ibid.*, p. 429.

94. *Ibid.*, p. 430.

95. *Ibid.*, Marshall to Talleyrand, April 3, 1798, p. 435.

96. *Ibid.*, pp. 436-37.

97. Incensed by a speech given in the House of Commons by the Attorney-General of England, Sir Roundell Palmer, concerning the reception of the Confederate ship, *Georgia*, in the port of Liverpool, George Bemis published *Precedents of American Neutrality*, in which he refuted Palmer's assertion that *le Cassius* was "received into the ports of the United States, held not to be amenable to courts of law, and never ordered by the Government to leave the port." George Bemis, *Precedents of American Neutrality* (Boston: Little, Brown and Company, 1864), p. 15. Bemis contended that the United States had honored its duty as a neutral nation and that *le Cassius* was condemned

and forfeited. There is no record of the forfeiture, but Bemis based his argument on the words of Justice Johnson in an 1816 case. "In the case of The Cassius, which belonged to the French republic, the vessel was finally prosecuted and condemned on an information *qui tam*, under the act of Congress for an illegal outfit, and thus had applied to her, under the statute, the principle . . . with relation to a private armed vessel." 1 Wheaton 238, 252 (1816). Bemis surmised that the forfeiture was the outcome of the third action. The reporter in the second case, *Ketland v The Cassius*, 2 Dallas 365 (1796), noted in a footnote that "counsel for the prosecution said that he should commence a new (third) action." *Id.* at 369. Marshall's narrative ended with the decision in the second case.

98. Stinchcombe and Cullen, ed., *The Papers of John Marshall*, vol. 3, p. 439.

99. *Ibid.*, p. 440.

100. *Ibid.*, p. 443.

101. *Ibid.*, p. 445.

102. *Ibid.*, p. 446.

103. *Ibid.*, p. 445.

104. *Ibid.*, p. 447.

105. *Ibid.*, p. 445.

106. *Ibid.*, p. 451.

107. Stites, *John Marshall, Defender of the Constitution*, pp. 7-13.

108. Leonard Baker in his biography of John Marshall suggested that Marshall's interest in the law sprang from the fact that his family's interests were in land and that landowners depended so much on the law to protect them in their property rights. Baker, *John Marshall: A Life in Law*, pp. 7-10.

109. Journal entry of March 26, 1798, Stinchcombe and Cullen, ed., *The Papers of John Marshall*, vol. 3, p. 234.

110. *Ibid.*, Marshall to Washington, October 24, 1797, p. 268.

111. *Ibid.*, Marshall to Edward C. Carrington, September 2, 1797, pp. 123-24.

112. *Ibid.*, pp. 124, 126.

113. *Ibid.*, Marshall to Washington, September 15, 1797, p. 139.

114. *Ibid.*, Marshall to Mary W. Marshall, August 3, 1797, p. 122.

115. Responding to General Washington's urgings "to immediately set up some proper courts for the decision of Property and the legallity [*sic*] of Seizures: otherwise I may be involved in inextricable difficulties," the First Continental Congress passed resolutions on November 25, 1775, authorizing courts to exercise prize jurisdiction and providing in the seventh resolve for the distribution of proceeds: "Captures by privateers would be for the use of the owners of the vessel. The owners could make their own arrangements for dividing the prizes with their masters and crews. If the vessel making the capture was fitted out at the expense of one of the colonies, one-third would be for the use of the captors and two-thirds for the use of the colony. (Congress soon dropped this provision and allowed the colonies to decide for themselves the

proportion of the prize to be awarded to the master and crews of vessels which the various colonies paid to equip.)" Congress took two-thirds if it fitted out the vessel. Henry J. Bourguignon, *The First Federal Court: The Federal Appellate Prize Court of the American Revolution* (Philadelphia: The American Philosophical Society, 1977), p. 44-46. See also Jessup and Deak, "Early Prize Court Procedure," *Neutrality*, vol. 1, pp. 201-48.

116. Congress was empowered "To declare war, grant letters of marque and reprisal, and make rules concerning captures on land and water." Article I, section 8. Under the Articles of Confederation, the states were prohibited from granting "commissions to any ships or vessels of war, [and] letters of marque or reprisal, except it be after a declaration of war by the united states in congress assembled, and then only against the kingdom or state and the subjects thereof, against which war has been so declared." Article VI. The Congress was given "the sole and exclusive right and power of determining on peace and war" and "of establishing rules for deciding in all cases, what captures on land or water shall be legal, and in what manner prizes taken by land or naval forces in the service of the united states shall be divided or appropriated—of granting letters of marque and reprisal in times of peace." Article IX.

117. White, *The Marshall Court and Cultural Change*, vols. 3 and 4, pp. 884-926. Privateering also continued to be utilized although abuses were often associated with the practice. The United States voluntarily imposed a restriction on privateering in the treaty with Prussia in 1785 when the parties agreed not to use privateers against each other. The practice fell into disfavour. On April 6, 1856, the ministers negotiating a peace for the Crimean War adopted the declaration: "Privateering is and remains abolished." Carlton Savage, *Policy of the United States . . .*, p. 381, n. 2. The United States refused to sign unless amendments were made. Secretary of State William L. Marcy expressed the concerns of the United States to the French minister: "It is, in the opinion of this government, to be seriously apprehended that if the use of privateers be abandoned, the dominion over the seas will be surrendered to those powers which adopt the policy and have the means of keeping up large navies." *Ibid.*, p. 389. See also H. W. Halleck, *Elements of International Law and Laws of War* (Philadelphia: J. B. Lippincott & Co., 1878), pp.175-78.

118. 1 Cranch 3, 41 (1801). See the report of the case in the preceding term, when the Court voted to hold the case over for a hearing before a fuller court as it was a case of first impression. *Talbot v. Amelia, Seeman, Claimant*, 4 Dallas 34 (1800). See also Claude A. Swanson, ed., *Naval Documents Related to the Quasi-War Between the United States and France*, (Washington: Government Printing Press, 1938), vol. 6, pp. 242-43 for an "outline of the leading features of the case." See p. 283 for a copy of the appointment of George W. Talbot as agent to settle the crew's claims against the ship.

119. The District Court of New York allowed salvage. The Circuit

Court, Judge Washington presiding, reversed. Washington's reasoning in the case is interesting. Washington failed to assume that the ship would have been condemned in a French court pursuant to the Decree because "such a proceeding would be in violation of the laws of nations, however consistent it might be with her own laws." Washington assumed that the French courts would refuse to enforce the decree in favor of the law of nations. Swanson, *Naval Documents* . . ., vol. 6, p. 243.

120. Salvage is the compensation allowed to persons by whose assistance a ship with cargo has been saved in whole or in part from impending danger. Note re Salvage *Stratton v. Jarvis*, 8 Peters 4 (1834), 8 L.ed. 846.

121. Stinchcombe and Cullen, ed., *The Papers of John Marshall*, vol. 3, pp. 381-82.

122. *Ibid.*, John Marshall to Charles Lee, March 4, 1798, pp. 395-96. Marshall noted in the Journal on February 6 and 7 that he pressed Mr. Gerry "on the subject of our letter concerning the decree" but he had not read it. *Id.* at 198. On February 18, he noted that he "offered [the letter] to Mr. Gerry to sign but he declined." *Id.* at 200. The letter also contained a demand for passports.

123. *Ibid.*, pp. 390-91.

124. 1 Cranch 103 (1801).

125. 1 Cranch 103, 110.

126. 1 Wheaton 304 (1816).

127. During the years of hostility, 95 prizes were taken, 70 ships were condemned for a value of $ 700,000. Haskins and Johnson, *Foundations of Power, John Marshall, 1801-1815*, vol. 2, p. 409, n. 8, citing G. Allen, *Our Naval War with France* (Boston, 1909), p. 222.

128. Haskins and Johnson, *Foundations of Power: John Marshall 1801-1815*, vol. 2, p. 414. The cases are *Murray v. The Charming Betsy*, 2 Cranch 64 (1804), (See ch. 2, pp. 33-36, *supra* for Marshall's opinion in this case.) *Little v. Barreme*, 2 Cranch 170 (1804), *Maley v. Shattuck*, 3 Cranch 458 (1806), and *Sands v. Knox*, 3 Cranch 499 (1806).

129. 3 Cranch 458 (1806).

130. 2 Cranch 458, 491.

131. 2 Cranch 170 (1804)

132. 3 Cranch 499 (1806).

133. 3 Cranch 499, 502.

134. Wheaton, *The Law of Maritime Capture and Prizes*, p. iii.

135. *Ibid.*, p. v.

136. *Letters by Historicus on Some Questions of International Law* (London: Macmillan and Co., 1863). Sir William Vernon Harcourt, Q.C. (1827-1904), British statesman who embraced international law as his passion, not his profession, wrote the letters under the pseudonym, "Historicus."

137. *Ibid.*, p. vii.

138. *Ibid.*

139. *Ibid.*, pp. vii-viii.

# 4

# United States Representative

John Marshall served in the House of Representatives during the first session of the Sixth Congress. The importance of foreign policy was indicated by President John Adams's letter to members of the cabinet requesting their opinions on subjects he planned to include in his speech to Congress in December of 1799. He specifically asked for opinions on "the state of Europe, the mission to France, . . . the negotiations with St. Domingo, [and] the interruption of the board or boards of commissioners [under Articles VI and VII of the Jay Treaty]."[1] Marshall arrived in Philadelphia after a vigorous campaign and a close election to represent Virginia in a Congress deeply involved with questions of international relations.

His return to the United States after rejection by the French Directory and his decision to run for a seat in the House of Representatives in 1799 led to his eventual decision to abandon law practice and remain in Washington. Significantly, the XYZ mission temporarily helped the Federalist party, but it could not counteract the negative effect of the Alien and Sedition Acts passed by the Federalist Congress to silence political opposition. During the elections of 1799, the popularity Marshall gained from the mission to France was not sufficient to guarantee his election. He had to work hard to be elected, a stark contrast to his state election experience. In 1795, Marshall had been elected to the Virginia House of Delegates, although he refused to run and was not even aware that he was a candidate until informed of his election.[2]

During the congressional campaign, newspaper attacks against Marshall intensified, concentrating on his down-the-line support of the administration's foreign policy. Typical of the Republican tactics were those employed by John Thompson, who as "Curtius" attacked Marshall for being willing to "sell American independence to British merchants" in order to enrich the few.[3] Marshall was soundly denounced for being pro-British by the *Richmond*

*Examiner*, the leading Republican newspaper. Support for his candidacy came from the short-lived Federalist organ, the *Virginia Federalist*. Marshall ran against John Clopton of New Kent County, an incumbent who had been elected to the Fourth Congress in 1795.

Soon after Marshall announced for Congress, he published his stand on the issues he considered most important by answering questions posed in the press by one "Freeholder."[4] Four of the five questions concerned foreign policy. The only question not relating to foreign policy was whether Marshall subscribed to the principles of the Constitution. The "Freeholder" asked about neutrality, the Jay Treaty, the United States' relations with Great Britain and France and Marshall's opinion on the Alien and Sedition Acts. Marshall endorsed the policy of neutrality but broke with the national leadership of his party by opposing the Alien and Sedition Acts, pledging his vote against any attempt to renew them. Using language that echoed Washington's Farewell Address and foreshadowed Jefferson's first Inaugural Address, Marshall neatly summarized his foreign policy credo: "The whole of my politics respecting foreign nations are reducible to this single position. We ought to have commercial intercourse with all, but political ties with none. Let us buy cheap and sell as dear as possible. Let commerce go wherever individual, and consequently national interest, will carry it; but let us never connect ourselves politically with any nation whatever."[5]

Marshall's views on foreign policy were reiterated in a letter to General Thomas Posey in 1799, with whom he served at Stony Point, New York, during the Revolution. The importance of his views to his subsequent work on the Court warrants quoting them fully:

> I had stated that America ought to view all foreign nations with an equal eye. That we ought to assure ourselves that no nation ever had or ever woud have any regard for us—that they woud regulate themselves entirely by their own interest & that we ought to think so. That we were in the habit of expressing immense affection & gratitude for France & unlimited hate for Britain. Yet at a very critical period the conduct of those two nations towards us had been such as ought to induce to consider them as exactly equal—without favor to either. That while France was our friend, our ally, & united with us in a common war the use she made of her influence was to endeavor to deprive us of our western country & of the navigation of the Mississippi . . . that Britain our foe, the instant she determind on peace acknowledgd our independence & ceded to us a share in the fisheries. That this was not produced by the friendship of Britain or the hostility of France but by a political regard on the part of each on its own interest.[6]

Marshall strongly supported the policies adopted during Washington's administration. With the exception of the Alien and Sedition Acts, he based his campaign firmly on the side of the Adams administration, even though Federalism in Virginia was clearly on the decline. On January 8, 1799, he told Washington that he was uncertain about the outcome of the election, but that he felt he had taken the proper course:

> Whatever the issue of the election may be I shall neither reproach my self nor those at whose instance I have become a candidate, for the step I have taken. I feel with increasd force the obligations of duty to make sacrafices & exertions for the preservation of American union & independence, as I am more convinc'd of the reality of the danger which threatens them. . . . If I fail I shall regret the failure more on account of the evidence it will afford of the prevalence of a temper hostile to our government . . . than of the personal mortification which woud be sustained.[7]

Marshall was elected by a margin of 108 votes, a victory perhaps determined by Patrick Henry's last minute support. In the political battleground of Virginia, he was a Federalist who could win "in spite of [his] support for the federal government."[8] The ephemeral popularity resulting from the XYZ affair, which helped him take his seat in the Sixth Congress, did not aid the Federalist candidate for the same seat in the next election. When he resigned after the first session, his replacement, Littleton Waller Tazewell, a Republican, was swept in on the rising tide of Republicanism. On August 5, 1800, Marshall told Harrison Gray Otis, "Ill news from Virginia. To succeed me has been elected by an immense majority one of the most decided democrats in the union."[9]

Marshall served in the House for only six months. That his diplomatic experience in France influenced his work can be observed by a review of his participation in House business. Since 1793, when he "joined the [political] battle"[10] to support the President's Proclamation of Neutrality, Marshall had examined national prospects and problems as they existed in an international context. In Virginia, he "was virtually the only Virginia Federalist who could see beyond the immediate issues and view the struggle as one of national vs. local, parochial interests."[11] In Washington, the view was international.

The Sixth Congress convened on December 2, 1799 in Philadelphia. During the session, which adjourned on May 14, 1800, Marshall proved to be an able and active legislator. He also exhibited an independence that alienated many of the more partisan Federalists. Not only was Marshall present to vote on issues at roll call (missing only 6 votes),[12] he served on committees, some as chairman. Although Jefferson reported at the close of the session that the Federalists (even with a majority of twenty) had not been able "to carry a single strong measure in the lower house,"[13] a contemporary summary of the session's business indicated that the legislators were indeed busy with substantive matters, the bulk of which concerned foreign affairs. The business included reducing military appropriations for the army to $ 3,042,576 by stopping enlistments, and reducing naval appropriations to $ 2,500,000 by suspending construction on frigates. Bills were introduced and passed to better govern the navy, to regulate public arsenals and magazines, to provide for a uniform system of bankruptcy, to conduct the second census, to effectuate removal of the public offices from Philadelphia to Washington, D.C., to divide the Northwest Territory, to accept the cession by Connecticut of Western Reserve lands, to suspend commercial intercourse with France and her dependencies, to defend merchant vessels against French depredations, and to extend the act prohibiting United States citizens from hostile acts on neutral nations and from accepting commissions in foreign service for that purpose.[14]

Beveridge recounts Marshall's leadership positions in Congress. Marshall drafted the House response to President Adams's address at the beginning of the session. Within two weeks after the Congress convened, he announced the death of Washington and introduced resolutions penned by Henry Lee to commemorate his death. He chaired the committee and authored the bill accepting the Western Reserve land. Marshall led the drive to keep the military court jurisdiction over Marine Corps officers, and for land grants to Revolutionary War veterans.[15] Beveridge reported that Marshall took a "leading and determining part" in the five important issues before the house:[16]

1. True to his campaign statement, Marshall voted to repeal offending sections of the Sedition Act. His vote was important in the 50-48 count for repeal.[17]

2. Through amendment and debate, Marshall effectively defeated the Disputed Elections Bill favored by the Federalists.[18] The bill provided for a committee composed of six senators, six representatives and the Chief Justice of the Supreme Court to receive the electoral votes after they were opened in the House and read to Congress. The committee, in secret, would exercise absolute, unappealable authority to determine the validity and the regularity of the votes.[19]

3. Marshall served as a member of the committee to report a National Bankruptcy law, and was instrumental in crafting the provisions requiring a jury to decide the fact of bankruptcy and the provisions restricting the means to cure bankruptcy.[20]

4. Marshall defended the President's action in extraditing Thomas Nash, alias Jonathan Robbins, under Article XXVII of the Jay Treaty.[21]

5. Marshall successfully opposed the attempts by the Republicans to reduce the size of the Army.[22]

He showed intense interest in the last two issues, which involved foreign affairs. On both of these issues, he spoke at length. In the dispute over the Nash/Robbins extradition, Marshall seized the opportunity to construe the meaning of Article XXVII of the Jay Treaty to support Adams's delivering him up to British authorities.

Thomas Nash, in 1791, was serving as a crew member on the British frigate *Hermione*. The crew mutinied, killed the officers, and took the boat into a Spanish port. In 1799, the British consul had Nash arrested in Charleston, South Carolina, for murder and applied to the local authorities and then to the President for extradition. President Adams wrote to the District Judge in Charleston, Judge Bee, ordering him to determine if there was sufficient cause to try the accused and, if so, to deliver him to the British authorities. Under a writ of habeas corpus, Nash appeared for a hearing before the District Judge who found sufficient evidence to try him and, therefore, ordered him delivered to the captain of the British sloop *Sprightly*, then in the Charleston harbor. Nash was subsequently court martialed and hanged.[23]

The House began debate on resolutions introduced by Edward Livingston, Republican from New York, on February 20, 1800, condemning President Adams's handling of the affair. The Republicans were incensed by what they considered an unwarranted exercise of authority by the "monarchical" Adams. Nash contended that he was an impressed American seaman from Danbury, Connecticut. Republicans tended to credit his story, although there was evidence to prove Nash was an Irishman subject to British jurisdiction. They faulted the president for impinging on the judicial branch by deciding the following questions of law: (1) whether the offence was committed within British jurisdiction; (2) whether the crime committed was comprehended by the treaty.[24]

Marshall admitted that the president might have decided the legal issues, but he denied that the questions were "improper for executive decision." Marshall reasoned that the case for extradition depended on the truth of three propositions, which he sought to prove: (1) The case was covered by Article XXVII of the Jay Treaty; (2) The question was therefore properly one for the executive, not the judiciary; and (3) The president had not interfered with a judicial decision.

Marshall grounded his defense of the President in the law of nations and in Article XXVII of the treaty. The offences, mutiny and murder, were committed upon the high seas aboard a British vessel. Marshall cited Thomas Rutherford's *Institutes of Natural Law*[25] for the proposition that "no nation has any jurisdiction at sea, but over its own citizens or vessels, or offences against itself."[26] Marshall recognized that jurisdiction over persons or vessels on the high seas was determined by ownership and citizenship. Britain's jurisdiction extended to its citizens and property, although outside its territorial jurisdiction. The Republicans had argued further that the crime of mutiny was, by the laws of both the United States and Great Britain, an act of piracy, i.e. a crime against all nations.[27] Pirates were not protected from any jurisdiction and could be punished by all nations. The United States, therefore, did not have to extradite Nash/Robbins, as piracy was not comprehended by the treaty.[28] Marshall maintained that Nash was extradited not for piracy, but for murder, which was comprehended by the treaty. Further, the acts of mutiny and murder were crimes against the country of England specifically, not against the entire world, and as such were covered by Article XXVII:

> It is further agreed that His Majesty and the United States, on mutual requisitions, by them respectively, or by their respective Ministers or officers authorized to make the same, will deliver up to justice all persons who, being charged with murder or forgery, committed within the jurisdiction of either, shall seek an asylum within any of the countries of the other, provided that this shall only be done on such evidence of criminality as, according to the laws of the place, where the fugitive or person so charged shall be found, would justify his apprehension and commitment for trial.[29]

Having established that England had jurisdiction over its own citizens at sea, Marshall looked to the treaty and the Constitution to find the duty of the President to extradite the accused. He found that the

> department which is entrusted with the whole foreign intercourse of the nation, with the negotiation of all its treaties, with the power of demanding a reciprocal performance of the article, which is accountable to the nation for the violation of its engagements, with foreign nations, and for the consequences resulting from such violation, seems the proper department, to be entrusted with the execution of a national contract, like that under consideration.[30]

Marshall concluded that the president had acted properly as his duty required. Having determined that the accused should stand trial, he was given over to the authorities with jurisdiction to try him. Marshall's lengthy discourse addressed all objections to the president's actions and silenced the opposition. Realizing, however, an ambiguous element in the requirements under the treaty, the House "went into Committee [of the Whole] on the bill for carrying into effect the twenty-seventh article of the Treaty with Great Britain." Marshall prepared an amendment to the proposed bill which provided

> that on any requisition being made under this article, the testimony should be taken in writing and transmitted to the Secretary of State, and by him laid before the President of the United States, whose opinion should decide whether the matter was cognizable in any court of the United States, or whether the offender should be delivered up; if the former, that he should give directions to the Judge in whose district the offender was apprehended to proceed to trial according to law: if not, and the

> crime came under the treaty, that he should direct the Secretary of State to direct the Judge to make the delivery.[31]

Although Marshall did not develop his arguments against the reduction of the army as extensively, he argued that the armed forces, as a practical matter, should be maintained at the existing levels in order to provide adequate defense.

Proponents for disbanding the forces argued that maintaining them was useless because invasion was improbable under the current state of affairs and that maintenance was too costly. Marshall answered that it was impossible to conclude that invasion was "impracticable" as the "present state of Europe" was totally unknown, as were "the late decisive victories of France." He looked at the "relative situation" of the United States and France and found that they were "at war in fact though . . . it is not declared in form."[32] Marshall expressed his belief that the House was being asked to act without the necessary knowledge. Addressing the objection of cost, Marshall argued that expenses could be cut "without dismissing the troops already in active service." Marshall pushed successfully to keep the forces at their present level, to suspend enlistments, and to await the results of the negotiations pending in France.[33]

The House also handled two matters in the regular course of business that involved French-American disputes. As one of his minor duties, Marshall reported the resolution recommending that William Tazewell, secretary to Elbridge Gerry in the last days of his ministry in France, be compensated for expenses "incurred by him in consequence of his being captured on his return to his country."[34] The House also voted with only four nays (Republicans John Randolph of Virginia and Matthew Lyon of Vermont among them) to commend the commander of the *USS Constellation*, Thomas Truxton, for a gold medal for bravery exhibited in battle with the French frigate *La Vengeance*.[35]

Marshall's activities in the House involved both international issues on which lengthy debates developed and minor issues in which only personal preferences were expressed. The diehard Federalists were not impressed with his performance. He "failed to please" them in the beginning of the session when he delivered the House response to Adams's message.[36] On December 29, 1799, Oliver Wolcott wrote to Fisher Ames a biased appraisal of Marshall, which included the perceptive observation that he was "too much disposed to govern the world according to rules of logic."[37]

While in the House, as in the years preceding, Marshall exhibited his unique ability to construe treaties. As counsel in *Ware v. Hylton et al.*, in his defense of the Jay Treaty, in his evaluation of the treaties of 1778 with France and in the Nash/Robbins episode, Marshall had treated the international agreement as a contract in an attempt to give meaning to the intention of the parties and the clear words of the instrument. He continued to use this ability on the Supreme Court. In *United States v. Schooner Peggy* (1801),[38] one of the first opinions he wrote after becoming Chief Justice, Marshall relied on the precedent of *Ware* and, as judge, repeated what he, as an attorney, had prompted, "The Constitution of the United States declares a treaty to be the supreme law of the land."[39]

In 1809, Marshall returned to the question of rights under the Treaty of 1783, when a British creditor sought to revive an unexecuted mortgage on land in Maryland through the Maryland confiscation act of 1780. The act confiscated all property owned by British subjects, except debts. A writ of error was taken from the state supreme court of Maryland, but Marshall dismissed the case as not "arising under the treaty." Marshall explained: "Whenever a right grows out of, or is protected by, a treaty, it is sanctioned against all the laws and judicial decisions of the states; and whoever may have this right, it is to be protected. But if the person's title is not affected by the treaty, if he claims nothing under a treaty, his title cannot be protected by the treaty."[40]

Cases in which treaty provisions affected private rights in property came regularly before the Court. While in Congress, Marshall had developed an appreciation for the role played by municipal law in international affairs. He wrote opinions resolving disputed land titles under the treaties of acquisition, drawing on this knowledge. In one of the cases, *Foster and Elam v. Neilson* (1829),[41] Marshall wrote an extensive historical review of the various treaties between France, Spain, Great Britain and the United States concerning the land of Louisiana and Florida. Marshall determined the ownership of the petitioners by applying the treaty under which the United States took possession of the land.

Title to a parcel of land located in the Province of West Florida was initially granted to Jayme Joydra on January 2, 1804 by Juan Ventura Morales, intendent of the Spanish government at that time. On May 17, 1805, Joydra sold 6,000 arpents of the larger tract to Joseph Maria de la Barba who, on the same day, sold 3,000 arpents to Francoise Poinet. Poinet later sold the 3,000 arpents to James Foster and Pleasant Elam. The petitioners, Foster and Elam, argued that their title to the land was good because Spain had title and the grant was confirmed by the Adams-Onis treaty signed on February 22, 1819, although not finally ratified until two years later. Marshall addressed the question, "To whom did the country between the Iberville and the Perdido rightfully belong, when the title now asserted by the plaintiffs was acquired."[42]

After reviewing the various acts passed by Congress from 1803 to 1819, Marshall examined the treaty by which Spain ceded all territory east of the Mississippi, known as East and West Florida, but which provided that "all grants of land made before the 24th January, 1818" were "ratified and confirmed to the person in possession."[43] Marshall noted that Spain had consistently denied that they had given up West Florida in the Treaty of San Ildefonso in direct contradiction to the claim by the United States that West Florida had been ceded thereby to France and subsequently to the United States in April of 1803 by virtue of the Louisiana Purchase.[44]

Marshall concluded that the words of the treaty confirming grants made before 1818 did not act directly on the land, but left the confirmation of titles to Congress, which had established boards of commission to receive claims and determine title. He held that the Act of 1804 dividing Louisiana into two territories, annulling all grants in the ceded territory, invalidated the grant under which the claimants held title. As the claimants had not proved subsequent confirmation of title under the various Congressional acts, he dismissed their petition.

In his opinion, however, Marshall elaborated on the definition of a treaty: "A treaty is in its nature a contract between two nations, not a Legislative Act. It does not generally effect, of itself, the object to be accomplish, especially so far as its operation is infraterritorial; but is carried into execution by the sovereign power of the respective parties to the instrument. . . . and the Legislature must execute the contract before it can become a rule for the court."[45] International law controlled in defining treaty obligations whose operation was "extraterritorial" (i.e., in the relationship of nation with nation), but in treaties of acquisition, municipal law enacted by Congress controlled title to land. To hold otherwise would allow the ceding nation to control the land after the cession. Congress, in legislating title to the land, would be held to the terms of the treaty.

In a subsequent title dispute in the same area, Marshall observed that Spain's practice of ceding large grants of land to individuals began when the country decided to cede the Floridas to the United States, and that these grants had been considered frauds upon the United States. Marshall reasoned that even "admitting that the Spanish government was more liberal," the fact could not be used to invalidate titles, otherwise good, to which the United States had offered no objections.[46] Marshall confirmed the title of George Clarke who held under a grant from the Governor of the Province of East Florida. He reiterated the right of the state to exercise "political" control over the lands.[47]

In his last few months on the Court, Marshall delivered the opinion in a case of disputed title to a lot in the city of New Orleans.[48] He dismissed the case for lack of jurisdiction, holding that the effect of a treaty of cession ceased to operate when statehood began. Catherine Gonzales claimed title to the city lot under a Spanish grant; the city of New Orleans claimed title under a French grant. The Supreme Court of the State of Louisiana decided the controversy in favor of Gonzales. Marshall reasoned that Congress and consequently the Supreme Court had jurisdiction over the territory until statehood, at which time the sovereign power over state land passed to the state. Marshall noted that Gonzales held land to which the title had been confirmed under the laws of the United States and that a patent had been issued to her in 1821.

In the cases involving land ceded by treaty, Marshall recognized that the question of land title at some point became a political question, that is, one for another branch of the government to decide. He deferred to the legislative branch. In the Nash/Robbins debate, he recognized the right of the executive to exercise extradition under the Jay Treaty and worked in the legislature to formulate rules for the process. His basic understanding that treaties were not self-executing was derived from his experience.

Marshall's arguments in the Nash/Robbins debate presupposed an understanding of the law of piracy. However, he had endorsed the extradition of Nash/Robbins, insisting that Nash was indicted not for piracy, but for murder. Marshall defined general piracy as a crime against all nations, punishable by all; whereas, murder aboard the ship of a national was a crime against the nation, punishable under the nation's municipal statutes. To Marshall, the distinction was jurisdictional, and the jurisdiction of a nation's courts extended to its ships on the high seas. As Chief Justice, he wrote two opinions which emphasized jurisdiction as a principle consideration in defining piracy. In 1819, Marshall wrote to Bushrod Washington about a case in Richmond, indicating that the application of a municipal penalty in a case of general piracy somehow derogated from the international aspect of the crime.

> In the trial at Richmond the evidence was perfectly clear & the case was unequivocally a case of piracy according to the laws of every civilized nation. The doubt I entertain is whether there is any such thing as Piracy as "defined by the laws of nations." All nations punish robbery committed on the high seas by vessels not commissioned to make captures, yet I doubt seriously whether any nation punishes otherwise than by force of its own particular statute.[49]

Congress had enacted such a statute in 1790; and in 1818, the Supreme Court considered questions certified by the Massachusetts Circuit Court on the construction of the congressional act. In the statute, acts of piracy, robbery and murder, were designated "crimes against the United States." The punishment was death. Marshall noted that piracy was not a crime against the United States but a crime against all nations. The persons charged with piracy in Massachusetts were revolutionaries fighting a civil war against Spain, and Marshall concluded that revolting subjects could not be charged with piracy under the act.[50] Two years later, questions were certified from the Circuit Court of Virginia in *The United States v. Klintock* (1820), which involved an act of piracy committed aboard a Danish vessel, no longer under the control of the nation or its citizens. Marshall reiterated his opinion that, "the crime of robbery, committed by a person on the high seas, on board of any ship or vessel belonging exclusively to subjects of a foreign state, on persons within a vessel belonging exclusively to subjects of a foreign state is not a piracy within the true intent and meaning [of the congressional act of 1790]."[51] The act comprehended, however, acts "by persons on board of a vessel not at the time belonging to the subjects of any foreign power, but in possession of a crew acting in defiance of all law."[52]

Marshall found the distinguishing factor in the two cases to be that the vessel in the latter case was not controlled by a sovereign with jurisdiction over the accused. The courts of the United States could take jurisdiction over Klintock under the general law of nations and his punishment could be predicated on the Act of 1790. Marshall's reasoning in the two cases emphasized jurisdiction and the parallel to his argument in defense of extradition is apparent. Nash/Robbins's act occurred aboard a British vessel making him subject to British jurisdiction and extradition. Marshall distinguished between general piracy under the law of nations and piracy defined by municipal statute. Both were punishable by United States courts under municipal acts written by Congress with constitutional authority.

When Marshall left the first session of the Sixth Congress a few days before it ended, he took with him an increased understanding of how the law of nations functioned as a part of the law of the land. He worked for the first time in legislation that had an immediate impact on other nations. The size of the navy, the construction of frigates, military expenditures, appropriation of the western lands, and nonintercourse acts were daily concerns during his tenure. Under the Constitution, Congress was charged with duties affecting international relations and foreign policy.[53] Marshall learned the jurisdictional limits of the executive and the legislative in foreign matters. Adams had set the priorities for the House when he asked advice on international issues. In the treaty dispute, Marshall explored the jurisdictional limits between municipal legislation and international law. He studied both the municipal and international law of piracy.

Marshall left Philadelphia to be in Richmond to try cases when the Circuit Court opened.[54] Before he left, Adams, restructuring the Cabinet, offered him the post of Secretary of War. He declined. News reached him in Virginia that he had been confirmed as Secretary of War on May 9 and that three days later the Senate had received his nomination for Secretary of State. Marshall, considering the mixed blessings of public service over the past seven years, accepted the job at State with some misgivings.

## NOTES

1. George Gibbs, ed., *Memoirs of the Administrations of Washington and John Adams: From the Papers of Oliver Wolcott, Secretary of the Treasury* (New York: William Van Norden, Printer, 1846), vol. 2, Memorandum from President Adams, October 18, 1799, p. 298.

2. Beeman, *The Old Dominion and the New Nation, 1788-1801*, pp. 36-37. Beeman noted that Marshall did not rely on "liberal distribution of food and drink to potential supporters" in state elections.

3. *Ibid.*, p. 207. See also Baker, *John Marshall: A Life in Law*, pp. 303-14, and Beveridge, *The Life of John Marshall*, vol. 2, pp. 374-431 for complete accounts of the campaign.

4. There is reason to believe that Marshall posited the questions.

Both questions and answers were printed on October 20, 1798 in the *Columbian Centinel*, Boston, Massachusetts. Only the answers appeared in the *Times and Virginia Advertiser*, Alexandria, Va., Oct. 11, 1798. They are reprinted in Beveridge, *The Life of John Marshall*, vol. 2, Appendix III, pp. 574-77.

5. *Ibid.*, p. 576.

6. Cullen, ed., *The Papers of John Marshall*, vol. 4, Marshall to Thomas Posey, January 30, 1799, pp. 5-6.

7. *Ibid.*, Marshall to Washington, January 8, 1799, p. 4.

8. Beeman, *The Old Dominion and the New Nation*, p.88.

9. Cullen, ed., *The Papers of John Marshall*, vol. 4, Marshall to Harrison Gray Otis, August 5, 1800, p. 205.

10. Alexander DeConde, *Entangling Alliance: Politics and Diplomacy under George Washington* (Durham, N. C.: Duke University Press, 1958), p. 230.

11. Beeman, *The Old Dominion and the New Nation*, p. 157.

12. Beveridge, *The Life of John Marshall*, vol. 2, p. 445.

13. Gibbs, ed., *Memoirs of the Administrations of Washington and John Adams*, vol. 2, pp. 399-400, quoting Jefferson to Madison.

14. *Ibid.*, pp. 340-41. See also *Annals of Congress*, X, pp. 638 et seq.

15. Beveridge, *The Life of John Marshall*, vol. 2, pp. 446-48.

16. *Ibid.*, p. 451.

17. *Ibid.*, p. 451. See also Baker, *John Marshall: A Life in Law*, pp. 326-27.

18. Beveridge, *The Life of John Marshall*, vol. 2, pp. 455-58.

19. For a complete discussion of Marshall's role in this "high-handed attempt to control the coming presidential election," see Beveridge, *The Life of John Marshall*, vol. 2, pp. 452-58. See the committee report of April 25, 1800, on "An Act Prescribing the Mode of Deciding Disputed Elections of President and Vice-President of the United States" in Cullen, *The Papers of John Marshall*, vol. 4, pp. 138-45.

20. *Ibid.*, pp. 481-82. See also Baker, *John Marshall*, pp. 323-24.

21. Beveridge, *The Life of John Marshall*, vol. 2, pp. 458-76. Baker, *John Marshall*, pp. 322-23.

22. Beveridge, *The Life of John Marshall*, vol. 2, pp. 476-81.

23. William Draper Lewis, "John Marshall, 1755-1835," *Great American Lawyers: A History of the Legal Profession in America* (Philadelphia: The John C. Winston Co., 1907), vol. 2, pp. 313-408 at 340-41.

24. Cullen, ed., *The Papers of John Marshall*, vol. 4, p. 103.

25. Thomas Rutherford, an Englishman, published his lectures on Grotius in *Institutes of Natural Law, Being the substance of a Course of Lectures on Grotius de Jure Belli et Pacis* . . . in 1754-1756. He was a member of the naturalist school, and Marshall had a copy of the *Institutes* in his library. See Ziegler, *The International Law of John Marshall*, pp. 8-9. See also Nussbaum, *A Concise History of the Law of Nations*, p. 164.

26. Cullen, ed., *The Papers of John Marshall*, vol. 4, p. 85.

27. *Ibid.*, p. 93.

28. *Ibid.*, p. 90.

29. Bemis, *Jay's Treaty*, p. 342.

30. Cullen, ed., *The Papers of John Marshall*, vol. 4, p. 105.

31. *Annals of Congress*, vol. 10, Sixth Congress, lst session, p. 654.

32. Cullen, ed., *The Papers of John Marshall*, vol. 4, p. 55. A report of Marshall's speech was printed in the Philadelphia *Aurora* on January 17, 1800. In Richmond, Samuel Pleasants, Jr., printed anonymously, "A Letter from Manlius, to John Marshall, Esq. Member of Congress" in February, which refuted Marshall's stand on this issue as well as registering a protest against the "depredations of the general government." *Id.* at pp. 53-58, 61-74 at 73.

33. *Ibid.*, p. 54, n. 1.

34. *Annals of Congress*, vol. 10, pp. 661, 673. The bill authorizing compensation passed on April 28, 1800. Timothy Pickering had written to the Committee objecting to payment as Tazewell stayed beyond the time authorized for compensation. Cullen, ed., *The Papers of John Marshall*, vol. 4, p. 162. As late as August 22, 1800, Tazewell, "anxious to bring the business to a conclusion on any terms," wrote to Marshall asking him how much he was to be paid. *Id.* at pp. 229-30.

35. *Annals of Congress*, vol. 10, pp. 640-42.

36. Beveridge, *The Life of John Marshall*, vol. 2, p. 434.

37. Wolcott to Ames, December 29, 1799, Gibbs, ed., *Memoirs of the Administrations of Washington and Adams*, vol. 2, p. 314.

38. 1 Cranch 103 (1801).

39. 1 Cranch 103, 109. See discussion of the case in ch. 3, pp. 70-71. For further discussion on Marshall's treaty cases, see Edward Dumbauld, "John Marshall and Treaty Law," 50 *American Journal of Legal History* 69 (1956).

40. *Owings v. Norwood's Lessee*, 5 Cranch 344, 348 (1809).

41. 2 Peters 253 (1829).

42. 2 Peters 253, 300.

43. 2 Peters 253, 300.

44. The confusion of land title in this area was apparent in the division on the Court. Marshall noted that he and "one other judge" disagreed with the majority on the effect of the addendum to the treaty on small tracts of land.

45. 2 Peters 253, 314.

46. *United States v. Clarke*, 8 Peters 436, 462-63. (1834).

47. 8 Peters 436, 469.

48. *The Mayor of New Orleans v. DeArmas*, 9 Peters 224 (1835).

49. Marshall to Washington, Richmond, October 31, 1819, John Marshall Papers, Manuscripts and Rare Books Department, The Earl Gregg Swem Library, The College of William and Mary, Williamsburg, Virginia.

50. *United States v. Palmer*, 3 Wheaton 610 (1818).

51. 5 Wheaton 144, 151 (1820).

52. *Ibid.*, p. 152. For a full discussion of the cases on piracy, see White, *The Marshall Court and Cultural Change*, vols. 3-4, pp. 870-76.

53. Article I, section 8. Over half of the enumerated articles charge Congress with legislating in areas of international concern.

54. Marshall asked permission of the House to leave on May 8. *Journal of the House*, vol. 3, p. 702.

# 5

# Secretary of State

President Adams appointed Marshall Secretary of State as the result of an upheaval in his administration. Adams restructured his cabinet late in the spring of 1800 in order to rid it of those who, more loyal to Alexander Hamilton than to himself, had been undermining his policies.[1] He angrily confronted Secretary of War James McHenry on May 5 and accused him of subservience to Hamilton. On May 10, Adams requested the resignation of Secretary of State Timothy Pickering. McHenry resigned, but Pickering refused. On May 12, Adams discharged Pickering and placed Marshall's nomination before the Senate. The Senate confirmed the nomination on May 13. Thus, as Albert J. Beveridge writes, the "Federalist Cabinet was broken to pieces, and a presidential election was at hand which would settle the fate of the first great political party in American history."[2]

When the Federalist Party split, Marshall "bolted the party to stand with Adams" during the last months of his administration.[3] Marshall consistently endorsed both the Washington and Adams administrations, particularly in regard to foreign policy. The split within the party had an immediate impact on the election. Diplomatic historian Alexander DeConde concluded that "Adams's insistence on carrying out his policy of peace in defiance of the Hamiltonians helped turn the campaign of 1800 into a fierce, mudslinging battle in which the two wings of the Federalist party became more bitter in their denunciations of each other than in their attacks on the Republicans."[4]

Marshall left Philadelphia in early May to return to Richmond, where he found the political winds none too favorable.[5] He did not leave the capital, however, before he refused the position of Secretary of War. When he learned later that his nomination as Secretary of State had been confirmed, he carefully considered whether he should accept the assignment. He weighed his decision against the political fortunes of the Federalist party and his own personal position within the party. Marshall explained his dilemma:

> I had not been long in Virginia [in 1800] when the rupture between Mr. Adams and Mr. Pickering took place, and I was nominated to the senate as secretary of state. I never felt more doubt than on the question of accepting or declining this office. My decided preference was still for the bar. But on becoming a candidate for Congress I was given up as a lawyer, and considered generally as entirely a political man. . . . On the other hand, the office was precisely that which I wished, and for which I had vanity enough to think myself fitted. I should remain in it while the party remained in power; should a revolution take place it would at all events relieve me from the competition for Congress without yielding to my adversaries, and enable me to return once more to the bar in the character of a lawyer having no possible view to politics. I determined to accept the office.[6]

Marshall was compelled to accept the position out of political expediency, but it is also significant that he considered himself fully competent to fill the position. Active in the administration during the period when "foreign affairs dominated American politics," [7] Marshall was convinced that the foreign policy pursued by Adams was essential for national survival, and he based his objections to Jefferson and the Republicans largely on foreign policy grounds. He expressed this opinion to Hamilton during the election of 1800.

The Republicans won in the electoral college, but as a result of the tie between their presidential and vice presidential candidates, Jefferson and Aaron Burr, the election went to the House of Representatives. Marshall, although persuaded by Hamilton not to support Burr, still found "solid and immovable objection" to Jefferson's election: "His foreign prejudices seem to me totally to unfit him for the chief magistracy of a nation which cannot indulge those prejudices without sustaining deep and permanent injury."[8]

Marshall accepted the cabinet post confident that he would work in harmony with Adams. He, unlike his predecessor, deferred to Adams and implemented his policies without question. The correspondence between Adams and Marshall revealed the mutual respect and trust that characterized their relationship.[9]

Marshall's appointment was well accepted throughout the party. Secretary of Treasury Oliver Wolcott, one of the High Federalists who managed to retain his position during the Adams purge, expressed a favorable opinion of Marshall. "The removals of Mr. Pickering and Mr. McHenry were made in a moment of passion . . . I consider Gen. Marshall and Mr. Dexter [appointed to replace McHenry as Secretary of War] as more than secretaries—as state conservatores—the value of whose services ought to be estimated, not only by the good they do, but by the mischief they have prevented."[10]

Alexander DeConde summarized the many reasons why Marshall was a good choice:

> He was loyal to Adams, he was experienced in diplomacy, he had served in Congress, he was a personal friend of almost all Federalist leaders, and being from Virginia he would strengthen the Federalist party in the South. Even though Marshall had disapproved of the Alien and Sedition Acts, had dissented from High Federalist plans in Congress, and had supported the Ellsworth mission [to France], Federalist leaders trusted him.[11]

Marshall's tenure was not only brief, but it was also clouded by the political events preceding the election of 1800. During the first part of Marshall's tenure, which lasted nine months, the upcoming presidential election consumed Adams's interest. On December 3, 1800, electors in the various states met to choose the president and vice-president. Less than two weeks later, Hamilton wrote to Wolcott that it was then certain that either Burr or Jefferson would be President, and he expressed his preference for Jefferson.[12] It was not until February 17, 1801 that Jefferson, on the thirty-sixth ballot, was chosen President by the House.

Adams, aware of his upcoming defeat, had earlier nominated Marshall as Chief Justice to the Supreme Court on January 20, 1801. The Senate confirmed the nomination on January 27, and the commission was delivered on January 31. For the last four weeks of his nine months as Secretary of State, Marshall simultaneously held the office of Chief Justice.[13]

In spite of the brevity of his term and the political confusion, Marshall performed the job of Secretary of State to the satisfaction of the President, dealing with a wide range of international issues as well as with various mundane administrative chores. He began his duties in early June of 1800. After a briefing session, Adams left to spend the summer in Quincy. Beveridge contends that Marshall virtually ran the government during this period, even writing Adams's farewell address.[14] In addition to speech writing, Marshall was responsible for administrative duties, which included "the granting of patents, copyrights, and passports, the taking of the census, the recording of land patents, the supervision of the Mint (which had remained in Philadelphia), the printing and distributions of the laws of the United States, the preparation and delivery of commissions of appointment, and the large and complicated responsibility of supervising the territories of the United States."[15] Routine business also included the administration of justice and supervision of the commissioners in charge of constructing the new government buildings in Washington.

Although Marshall handled relatively few foreign policy issues during his short term, the issues that did arise involved a wide range of international law principles which were necessary to solve the disputes that came before him later on the Supreme Court. Marshall directed foreign policy by constantly conferring with Adams. The records indicate that he did not act alone even on minor appointments. Marshall's work on foreign policy involved United States' relations with France, Great Britain, and Spain. Insuring compliance with the treaties with the Barbary powers also required much of Marshall's time. An analysis of Marshall's activities in these four areas confirms the hypothesis that he was well schooled in international law.

### Relations with France

When Marshall began his duties as Secretary of State in June of 1800, the special envoys William Vans Murray, Oliver Ellsworth, and William R. Davie were already in Paris. Their first dispatch dated April 18, 1800, was not received until after Marshall assumed office. Adams had surprised his party in February of 1799 when he named the three men to a new peace mission. William Vans Murray, resident minister at The Hague, was already in Europe. Ellsworth and Davie sailed from Newport, Rhode Island, aboard the *United States* on November 3, 1799, arriving at Lisbon, Portugal, on November 27. The three did not reach Paris until March 2, 1800, approximately one year after they had received their commissions. While Ellsworth and Davie were crossing the Atlantic, Napoleon, on November 9, overthrew the Directorate and established himself as First Consul for a ten year term. When Secretary of State Pickering drafted the envoys' instructions on October 22, he stipulated that negotiations should begin within twenty days after their arrival in Paris and should be completed by April 1, 1800. Because of various delays, the negotiations began April 2, 1800, one day after the date set by Pickering for their completion.

The delay was not caused by French reluctance to negotiate. The dispatch of April 18 revealed that Talleyrand received the envoys on March 4, the day after they requested to be received. They were informed on March 5 that Napoleon would receive them March 17 at the Tuileries. On March 9, they were informed that they would be negotiating with three French ministers, Joseph Bonaparte, Napoleon's oldest brother, and Counsellors of State Pierre Louis Roederer and Charles Pierre Claret Fleurieu. The first dispatch included copies of two decrees, Napoleon's decree of March 4 instructing the French ministers to negotiate with the envoys and his decree of April 5 giving the ministers broader powers to negotiate. The second decree was in response to the envoy's concern expressed two days earlier that the French ministers' powers did not encompass all of the issues on which the envoys were instructed to negotiate.[16]

Marshall, on July 21, sent the deciphered dispatches from the envoys to Adams in Quincy, noting that he sent them hurriedly without copying them in order to avoid any delay. Marshall told Adams that:

> On the information given by these dispatches it woud be rash to form any decisive judgement respecting the issue of the embassy, but I am much inclind to think the negotiation will not speedily be terminated. The French government may be inclind to protract it in the expectation that the events of this campaign in europe & certain possible political events in America may place them on higher ground than that which they now occupy.[17]

Marshall's skepticism must be attributed to his own personal experience in France, as the dispatches revealed that the second mission was promptly received by the highest officials. Marshall nevertheless informed Pickering, "The intelligence from our envoys at Paris furnishes no data from which to infer either their success or failure."[18]

When Adams returned the papers to Marshall on July 31, he concurred in Marshall's assessment and expressed his opinion that naval protection of commerce should not be relaxed.[19] News from the envoys was slow in coming and sparse in content; and in August, Marshall expressed his opinion to Adams that "We ought not to be surprised if we see our envoys in the course of a month without a treaty."[20] Adams responded in agreement and added, "Nor should I be surprized if they should be loaded with Professions and Protestations of Love, to substitute for a Treaty."[21] Adams fidgeted:

> The state of Things will be so critical that the Government ought to be prepared to take a decided Part. Questions of Consequence will arise, and among others, whether the President ought not at the opening of the session to recommend to Congress an immediate and general Declration of War, against the French Republic. Congress has already in my Judgment as well as in the opinion of the Judges at Phyladelphia, declared War, within the meaning of the Constitution, against that Republic, under certain restrictions and Limitations.[22]

Marshall's response was cautious and reflected his hope that war would not be necessary:

> It is certainly wise to contemplate the event of our envoys returning without a treaty, but it will very much depend on the inteligence & assurances they may bring, what course sound policy will direct the United States to pursue. I am greatly disposd to think that the present government is much inclind to correct, at least in part, the follies of the past. Of these none were perhaps more conspicuous or more injurious to the french nation than their haughty & hostile conduct to neutrals. Considerable

> retrograde steps in this respect have already been taken & I expect the same course will be continued. Shoud this expectation not be disappointed there will be security—at least a reasonable prospect of it—for the future & there will exist no cause of war, but to obtain compensation for past injuries. This I am persuaded will not be deemd a sufficient motive for such a measure.[23]

The envoys, in a dispatch dated August 15, 1800, described their meeting with the French ministers on July 11, 1800, in which the French made known their refusal to give up their rights under the 1778 treaty to asylum in United States ports for privateers and to United States' guarantee of their possessions in the West Indies if they would have to agree at the same time, to pay for the depredations on property of United States citizens. The French argued that the two requirements were inconsistent, as the first was predicated on denying the treaty and the second on affirming the treaty. The envoys informed the Secretary that the negotiations would either need to be abandoned or their "instructions deviated from."[24]

On October 1, 1800, Murray wrote a brief note to the Secretary of State that the negotiations had "terminated [the previous] night in the signature of a Provisional Treaty of Amity and Commerce."[25] Murray sent the "whole history" of the mission with Ellsworth and Davie, who left Paris on October 4. Murray's letter did not reach the State Department until December 15, 1800, but Davie arrived with a copy of the Convention on November 12, 1800.

Marshall's role in the second mission was as different from his participation in the first as the second mission differed from the first in its success. As there is no evidence that he discussed any of the issues with the envoys, it is safe to conclude that he avoided being involved in the second mission except tangentially. His signature, as Secretary of State, appeared at end of the Treaty of Mortefontaine following the signature of President Adams under the date of February 18, 1801.

Although Marshall was not actively involved in the success of the second mission, he was informed by it. As Secretary of State, he completed his apprenticeship in diplomacy. Both missions were undertaken to defend the rights of the United States, under the law of nations, to trade freely as a neutral nation. Napoleon's eagerness to receive the second mission was a sharp contrast to the Directory's unwillingness to negotiate with the first mission.

The ministers had been instructed to accomplish at least three things; (1) United States claims of spoliation were to be acknowledged, (2) France was to pay for the damage done to United States commerce, and (3) the United States was to be relieved of her obligations under the 1778 treaties with France. Although the ministers were able to accomplish only the third objective, they obtained a peace treaty ending the Quasi-War and explicitly recognizing the rights of the United States to trade as a neutral nation.

Included in the treaty were the neutral principles that free ships made free goods, that neutrals could trade freely with and between belligerents, and that blockades to be effective must be physical. The definition of contraband under the treaty was narrow, excluding foodstuff and naval stores. Alexander DeConde concluded that Napoleon negotiated the treaty hoping to use the United States as a neutral nation to his own advantage. France needed the neutral nations to trade. By negotiating fairly with the United States, France identified itself with "the cause of neutral rights" and at the same time encouraged the "Baltic powers to stand firm against British domination."[26] DeConde noted that, one week after the treaty was signed, Napoleon moved to form a League of Armed Neutrality to help him fight England. "Napoleon hoped to bring the United States and the European neutrals into the final phase of a war that would crush England and enable him to take over Louisiana in peace."[27]

Marshall received a letter from the minister to Spain, David Humphreys, noting that "Gen. Louis-Alexandre Berthier [had] arrived in Madrid from France and that he had spoken to the general."[28] Neither American was aware at the time that the purpose of the visit was to negotiate the retrocession of Louisiana to France as part of Napoleon's plan for acquiring an American empire.[29] While Marshall was Secretary of State, the armed league was formed on December 16, 1800, by Sweden, Denmark-Norway, Prussia and Russia, a league patterned, as the "Premier Consul had planned" on the Treaty of Mortefontaine.[30] To support the principles of neutrality, the neutral powers planned mutual convoys and agreed to back each other against offending belligerents.

## Relations with the Barbary States

Early in his tenure at State, Marshall received through John Quincy Adams, minister to Berlin, a proposition from Sweden to participate in armed convoys in cooperation with Sweden and Denmark for mutual protection against the Barbary powers in the Mediterranean. In his letter, John Quincy Adams mentioned that the United States "had submitted to an expense much greater than had ever been applied to that purpose by any european power."[31] Marshall, after consulting with the President, informed John Quincy Adams that the President was "far from being pleased with the State of our affairs with the Barbary powers: but he conceives that the engagements of the United States, tho' unreasonably burthensome, ought to be performed. He is not satisfied that in the existing state of those engagements, good faith will permit us to unite with other powers, in appointing, in concert with them, convoys for their and our trade." Marshall noted, however, that there was "cause to apprehend that the Barbary powers or some of them, will break their treaties with us, and recommence hostilities on our Commerce." In that event, the president, Marshall said, would be "well disposed" to enter into "reasonable arrangements with Sweden and Denmark."[32] The treaties to which Marshall alluded had been negotiated with the Barbary powers, Morocco, Tunis, Tripoli, and Algiers between 1791 and 1799.[33]

Problems with the Barbary powers first surfaced after the Revolution when the United States lost the protection of the British. Both John Adams and Thomas Jefferson had grappled with the matter of buying peace from the Barbary corsairs—Adams while peace minister in Paris in 1783 and, later, as minister to England in 1786 and Jefferson while minister to France in 1786. The two men made a joint report to Secretary of Foreign Affairs John Jay on March 28, 1786, after conferring in London. As a result of the report, Jay suggested to the Confederation Congress that the terms of a treaty with Algiers should be left to Adams and Jefferson.[34] Although treaties were attempted during this period, a naval force was thought necessary for security. President Washington, in his message to Congress in 1796, urged the gradual creation of a navy, "To secure respect to a neutral flag requires a naval force. . . . Our trade to the Mediterranean, without a protecting force, will always be insecure."[35] Congress in response commissioned the construction of six ships but provided in the act that the plans would be dropped if a treaty with Algiers was negotiated. The treaty was signed in 1797; and only three of the ships were completed, the *USS United States*, the *USS Constitution* and the *USS Constellation*, which were also launched in 1797.

Through treaty stipulations, the United States was obligated to purchase the right to use the Mediterranean. Marshall's correspondence with Israel Whelen, purveyor of goods, revealed constant efforts to purchase cargos and equip ships to satisfy these obligations. Marshall expressed his frustration and contempt to the United States Consul at Tunis, William Eaton, for the practice of purchasing neutral rights:

> The President has, but with very much reluctance consented to direct the purchase of the jewels. The exorbitant & unwarrantable demands of the barbary powers sit very uneasy on us & are submitted to with difficulty. For the jewels meerly we are unwilling to go to war & thus lose the benefit of the heavy expenses already incurd. But this system of heavy exaction must not be continued. You must persevere in your endeavors so long as you may safely do so, to avoid entirely or diminish this demand.[36]

No solutions were reached concerning the Barbary powers while Marshall was Secretary. He was harried by the need to satisfy the tribute demanded in the treaties, and he added his voice to others who decried the system. On July 29, 1800, he wrote to Consul General Richard O'Brien, frustrated by the inexactness with which matters were handled:

> I find it difficult from the papers in this Department to ascertain the precise state of our accounts with the Barbary powers. I

> shall be much obliged to you and to Consuls Eaton and Cathcart to make out a perfect and complete statement, if you have it in your power, to do so, shewing the claims of the different regencies, and the produce and application of every cargo which has arrived, and exhibiting also with precision the present state of their demands.[37]

O'Brien's reply explained the confusion, but did nothing to clarify the situation:

> On the 17th Ins arrived her the U S Ship [George] *Washington* Capt Bainbridge, when I had the honour of receiveing yrs of the 29th July. We are upwards. of 110 thsd. dollars in debt. to the Bacris & Busnach. of Algiers. we are. nearly 2 years in Arrears in our annuities to the regency — I am sorrow to find that few articles is sent on the Annuities and. no Cash to pay our debts. we should be More punctual. if not we shall experience difficulties. you had full statemt. of our affairs in The last dispatches you recd. from Capt. Smith. Copies of the dispatches of last year you shall have. again by the first Conveyance. but one Cargo of our stipulations to Tunis is forwarded & Tripolia *demands* an extra present. our Barbary affairs requires great attention the[y] have been much neglected.
> The dey has, demanded that the Ship [George] *Washington* should carry the presents of the Regency to Constantionople. I have tryed all in My power to evade this. but. I am affraid I shall be obliged to give way to prevent extraordinary difficulties We shall want 400 yds. of fine Cloth of 4 Colours for our 2 yrs. present in Sept. next it should be sent with *speed*.[38]

Marshall estimated to Congressman Roger Griswold, chairman of the House Ways and Means Committee, that tribute for 1801 would probably cost $ 288,886., and suggested that Congress appropriate no less than the requested sum, which admittedly was not an exact figure.[39] Shortly thereafter, he wrote a department memoranda noting that burdensome problems with the Barbary states required "immediate attention" and that "mischief from Tripoli" should be expected.[40] Approximately three months later, on May 10, 1801, the pasha of Tripoli declared war on the United States. The United States, under Jefferson's leadership, resorted to force to assure their rights to use the sea. The peace treaty signed in June of 1805 was not conclusive. The need to keep a naval force in the Mediterranean was urged in presidential messages into the 1830s, although trouble with the Barbary powers effectively ended with the peace of December 23, 1816.[41]

## Relations with Great Britain

Marshall made a thorough statement on relations with Great Britain in a letter of instructions to the United States minister in London, Rufus King, on September 20, 1800. He emphasized that the breakdown of negotiations over British debts under Article VI of the Jay Treaty was "attributable exclusively to the wild, extensive, and unreasonable"[42] construction of the article by the British Commissioners and that the "probability of negotiating with France" had no influence on the Commissioners.[43]

Marshall discussed United States' grievances against Great Britain for depredations on commerce under three "heads": (l) the construction given to the definition of contraband in the Jay Treaty; (2) the extent given to the rule concerning blockaded ports; and (3) the unjust decisions of the British Courts of Vice Admiralty which allowed prize to captures made without probable cause.[44]

As to contraband, Marshall noted that articles of war were universally considered to be contraband by the law of nations. As to "articles of promiscuous use," circumstances determined the nature of the particular article. The articles of contraband enumerated in the Jay Treaty included one provision which Marshall contended the British were using to extend the objects subject to confiscation. The provision defined contraband to include "generally whatever may serve *directly* to the equipment of vessels." Marshall noted that "no operation is referred to the word, 'directly.' . . . .Expunge it from the sentence and, according to [the British], the sentence will remain the same. . . . To exclude it, or to construe it as if it were excluded, is to substitute another agreement for that of the parties."[45] Marshall argued that the rules for construction of a compact (i.e. treaty) required that proper weight be given to important words to ascertain the meaning of the contracting parties.

He argued further that under the true meaning of contraband, only "promiscuous" goods intended for an enemy port were included. The British confiscated and condemned all goods bound for New Orleans, considering it to be an enemy port. Marshall argued that the port could not be legally considered an enemy port as it was by treaty with Spain "a place of deposit for merchandise and effects of [United States] citizens." As New Orleans was in fact a neutral port, all goods including those used to equip vessels should be exempt from confiscation. New Orleans was, according to Marshall,

> well known not to be a port usually resorted to for [the equipment of vessels]. The Spaniards do not there build or equip vessels, nor has it ever been a depot for naval stores. When then a vessel bound for New Orleans, containing a cargo proper for the ordinary use of those citizens of the United States who are supplied through that port, & evidence that it is designd for them, shall be capturd, such cargo is not "a just object of confiscation" altho a part of it shoud also be deemd proper for "the equipment

> of vessels,' because it is not "attempted to be carried to an enemy."[46]

Marshall contended that the British practice of declaring blockades subjected the "commerce of neutrals" to "universal capture" and that, during temporary absences of a blockading fleet, the commerce to the port should be free. Marshall thus insisted that blockades be actual and continuous to be effective.

In his most scathing criticism, Marshall blamed the practice of Vice Admiralty courts, condoned by the government, for unjustified depradations on United States commerce. Marshall noted that the courts, "whatever may be the case, seldom acquit[ted], and, when they [did], costs and damages for detention [were] never awarded."[47] Illegal captures were thus treated with impunity and condoned by the British courts. Marshall denounced the lack of justice and "respect for law" in the courts of the Vice Admiralty:

> The most effectual restraint is an upright judiciary which will decide impartially between the parties, & uniformly condemn the captor in costs & damages, where the seizure has been made without probable cause. If this practice be not honestly & rigidly observd, there will exist no restraint on the captors. Their greediness for gain will be checkd by no fear of loss, & indiscriminate captures will, consequently, be made. If the vessel shoud be adjudgd good prize, of which before an unjust tribunal there is, in all cases, considerable probability, the profit is theirs; if the vessel even be acquited, the loss falls entirely on the capturd. [The neutral merchant's] voyage becomes not only unprofitable but injurious to him.[48]

Marshall then discussed the British practice of impressment. Marshall noted that the "valuable class of men," United States seamen, were "composed of natives and foreigners." Britain claimed the right to impress its own subjects and had not disclaimed the right to impress citizens of other countries. Marshall denied emphatically the right of Britain to impress United States citizens. "The case of British subjects, whether naturalized or not," he found "more questionable," but "the right even to impress them [was] denied." The summary nature of impressment made it a practice to be universally condemned, although its onerous nature was more apparent in the case of United States citizens and alien seamen:

> Alien seamen, not British subjects, engaged in our merchant service, ought to be equally exempt with citizens from impressments: we have a right to engage them, and have a right to, and interest in, their persons, to the extent of the service contracted to be performed. Britain has no pretext of right to their persons

> or their service. To tear them, then from our possession, is at the same time an insult and an injury. It is an act of violence for which there exists no palliative.[49]

Marshall acknowledged the British argument that British subjects were not easily distinguishable from United States citizens but expressed doubt that any real difficulty existed. He contended that "among that class of people who are seamen," a "native American" and a "person raised to manhood in Great Britain or Ireland" were easily distinguishable by the United States, adding: "We do not perceive any reason why the capacity of making this distinction should not be possessed in the same degree by one nation as by the other."[50]

Marshall's position unequivocally condemned the practice. He found the procedure legally indefensible. It was a summary procedure without adequate provisions protecting the rights of the suspected. Marshall did not consider the legal position of Great Britain on the right of expatriation. Britain denied the right based on the doctrine of indefeasible allegiance. The British held that a British subject could not by legal or other means lose or deny his obligations as a citizen.

The practice of impressment by the British was initially restricted to United States vessels lying in British ports, "but by 1797 [the British] had extended the use of press gangs to ships on the high seas."[51] The United States government issued certificates of citizenship to crews, but these certificates were ignored and abuses attended their issuance. Marshall consistently denied the right of impressment and, as his discussion of the issue in the letter of instructions to King revealed, his opposition led him to deny even the slightest justification.

Increased depredations on United States commerce by the British prompted Rufus King to inquire into the cause. He ascribed the increase to uncontrolled plunder on the seas. Writing to Marshall on September 30, 1800, he concluded, "The result of my Enquiries satisfies me that . . . these increased irregularities proceed from the unchecked and base spirit of Plunder that influences so many of the English naval commanders."[52] Marshall shared this conviction and again faulted the Vice Admiralty courts for being "organizd for the purpose of legalizing plunder. . . ."[53]

Marshall instructed King at various times on the government's position in the ongoing negotiations concerning payment of the pre-Revolutionary War debts owed British creditors.[54] The commission set up in Article VI to hear and settle British claims had disbanded in July 1799. Marshall personally preferred to solve the arbitration commission's impasse by adopting formal "explanatory articles" providing rules of procedure and defining precisely the jurisdiction of the commission.[55] Until December of 1800, the administration entertained only two solutions to the problem, the use of explanatory articles and the payment of a lump sum. On December 4, 1800, Marshall advised King of yet another option. "The President directs me to inform you that an informal agreement, provided it be perfectly understood, will be satisfactory to this Government."[56] Marshall asked King for a report on the progress of the negotiations and listed the three options in form of preference:

> The most desirable plan of accommodation is by public explanatory articles, placing the treaty on its true principles, in terms not easily to be misunderstood. Second to this is the system of informal explanation. . . . If, in neither the one way nor the other, a new Board can be so constituted as to comply with the engagements we have made according to their real import, without exposing the United States to the immense losses threatened by that which has been dissolved, then the stipulation for a sum in gross will be deemed more eligible than to permit things to remain in their present unsettled situation.[57]

These instructions represented the last efforts of the Adams administration to settle the problems created by the Jay Treaty. Realizing that Adams had lost the election, Marshall wrote privately to King suggesting that he "delay" the negotiations and await news from the Jefferson administration on how to proceed. Marshall feared that an agreement based on his instructions might not be acceptable to the Republican administration.[58] Ten months after Marshall left the State department, King wrote to advise him of the substance of the Convention signed with Great Britain.[59] In his reply, Marshall praised King, "You have effected what, in America, has been hitherto deemd impracticable. You have made a treaty with one of the great rival nations of europe, which is not only acceptable to all, but the merit of which is claimed by both parties."[60]

Before leaving office, Marshall prepared and presented to the House of Representatives on February 27, 1801, an "account of the depredations committed on the commerce of the United States by vessels of Great Britain . . . since the commencement of the year 1800." In an accompanying letter, Marshall noted that "many captures have been made of which no complaint has been made to the Government."[61] The report covered the period immediately preceding Marshall's tenure and was given to Congress a week before the change of administrations in response to a resolution passed by the House on February 24 requesting the information. Marshall limited the report to 1800 and presented it hurriedly, considering the short amount of time left in the legislative session. To assure thoroughness, he attached letters from consuls and a letter from the president of the Philadelphia Chamber of Commerce to the Secretary of the Navy.

### Relations with Spain

On September 8, 1800, Marshall wrote a comprehensive statement of United States grievances against Spain addressed to David Humphreys, the United States minister in Madrid. Spain, an ally of France, infringed upon the neutral rights of the United States by allowing (1) the capture of [United States] merchant vessels by privateers, manned in whole or in part by Spaniards, and fitted out in Spanish ports, and (2) the condemnation of [United States] vessels, however captured, in the courts of Spain.[62]

Marshall contended that the first was a violation of Article XIV of the Pinckney Treaty and the second a violation of Article VI and that both were violations under the law of nations of the rights of neutrals. He noted that the privateers were commissioned in France and fitted out in Spanish ports to prey on United States ships in Europe and in the Caribbean and instructed Humphreys to make a "very serious remonstrance" against the practices.

Although Marshall recognized that the condemnations were made by French consular tribunals in Spain, he reasoned that condemnations of courts established with the consent of Spain were to be considered condemnations "made in the ordinary tribunals of the nation."[63]

Marshall recognized that France and Spain were allied in the war against England but insisted that Spain and the United States were neutrals as to each other and that their relationship was governed by their treaty and the law of nations. Under Article VI of the Pinckney Treaty, Spain was required to protect United States vessels brought to her ports by privateers and to "use all her efforts to recover and cause [the vessels and their effects] to be restored to the right owners."[64] Accordingly, Marshall instructed Humphreys to make a claim on the Spanish government to take effective measures to stop fitting out in their ports privateers commissioned to prey on United States commerce, to prevent condemnations in their ports of United States vessels and cargos, and to fully compensate the owners of vessels and cargoes for unlawful condemnations made within their jurisdiction.[65] Marshall departed from his usual position of presenting only general demands for compensation when he instructed Humphrey to negotiate also for payment of the specific claims of Henry Preble and Samuel and Miers Fisher. Marshall expected both general and specific compensation for depradations which he felt could be justified only if a state of war existed between Spain and the United States.[66]

In addition to the foreign policy issues in Europe, but related to Franco-American relations, Marshall performed administrative duties associated with St. Dominique. He received and forwarded to the President on August 30, 1800, the communication that Toussaint L'Ouverture had triumphed in the civil war in Saint Dominique against the mulatto Andre Rigaud.[67] One week later, Marshall sent Adams for his signature a proclamation that extended trade to the island of Hispaniola. Marshall enclosed also a letter from General Toussaint requesting that the United States open commerce with the island, adding that the heads of state were in agreement that trade should be open to the islands.[68] Marshall proposed the name of Bartholomew Dandridge, a merchant from Alexandria who had been secretary to Murray and King, for the position of consulate, should "this commerce . . . be extended."[69]

The proclamation signed under the date of Marshall's letter to Adams lifted the ban on trade imposed on the island by a congressional act of February 2, 1799, which suspended trade with France and her dependencies.[70] It opened trade with a dependency claimed by the French government and indirectly encouraged the revolt against France. The circumstances indicate that Marshall drafted the proclamation.

As Secretary of State, Marshall relied on Vattel, the authority recognized by the State Department.[71] He based his objections to Spain's conduct in his instructions to Humphreys on September 8, 1800, on the fact that the "agressions complained of are totally incompatible with those rules, which the law of nations prescribes for the conduct of a neutral power." On the manuscript, Marshall indicated his reliance on "Vat. Bk 3 S 15.95.97.102.104."[72] The sections are specific to the import of the instructions and cover the following topics: enlisting soldiers in foreign countries, the effect of giving assistance or allying with belligerents, the effect of assistance to a belligerent given by one not bound by treaty, the right of a neutral to war (without declaration) against a power assisting the enemy and the general conduct required of neutral nations. In his instructions to King on September 20, 1800, on the Jay Treaty negotiations, Marshall reasoned that the law of nations on contraband established "general principles" which should be particularized by treaty.[73] These instructions reveal not only a grasp of the principles of the law of nations, but also a discriminating use of those principles.

Marshall prepared on February 2, 1801, a memorandum on the state of foreign affairs as his successor would find them.[74] Three days earlier, while still performing his duties as Secretary of State, Marshall had been confirmed as Chief Justice of the Supreme Court. He remained in the position of Secretary of State for only one day after administering the oath of office to Thomas Jefferson on March 4, 1801. Until the arrival of James Madison as the new Secretary of State on May 2, 1801, Levi Lincoln served as acting Secretary of State.

## On the Court

Relinquishing his administrative duties on March 5, Marshall became a full-time jurist. In a myriad of fact situations over the period of his Chief Justiceship, Marshall applied the law of the rights and duties of neutrals that he had expounded as Secretary of State.

In *Rose v. Himely* (1808),[75] he wrote the opinion in a case involving trade with the islands of Santo Domingo which he as Secretary of State had been instrumental in declaring open. The Court entertained the question of the right of the French tribunal to issue condemnation of an American vessel engaged in trading with Santo Domingo. France had issued orders closing all ports in Santo Domingo except those not held by the insurgents, and asserted the right to condemn all vessels found within "two leagues of the coast" of the proscribed ports.[76] The United States schooner *Sarah* was siezed by a French privateer on February 23, 1804 as she left with a cargo picked up in Santo

Domingo. She was captured ten leagues from the coast, libeled in Cuba and sold before condemnation. The cargo was brought aboard the vessel the *Example* into the Charleston port. Rose, the supercargo in charge of the *Sarah*, followed the cargo and libeled the *Example* for its return.

Marshall recognized that a war de facto existed between France and Santo Domingo. The colony under Toussaint L'Ouverture had declared independence, and France was attempting to suppress the rebellion. Marshall reasoned that the Court must treat the problem as a civil war and recognize France's authority in the area. "It is for governments to decide whether they will consider Santo Domingo as an independent nation, and until such decision shall be made, or France shall relinquish her claim, courts of justice must consider the ancient state of things as remaining unaltered and the sovereign power of France over that colony as still subsisting."[77]

The ship had been captured pursuant to an act of municipal authority outside the limits of municipal jurisdiction. Marshall noted that municipal jurisdiction could not extend to international waters, the capture was therefore illegal. A strong dissent by Justice William Johnson was grounded on the "universal rule" that a "seizure on the high seas for a breach of blockade" was justified "during the whole voyage home."[78] Marshall did not find the blockade argument decisive. He found more persuasive the fact that "neither the vessel, nor the captain, supercargo, nor crew" had ever been brought within the jurisdiction of the courts of France but had been libeled in a neutral country. Marshall found that the sentence issued by "a court sitting in a neutral territory, and instituted by a belligerent" could not change title to the property.[79] Marshall held that the goods should be returned to the libelants, Rose and the owners, and remanded the case for further proceedings.

The "political relations between the United States and France" prompted the Court to call the case of *The Schooner Exchange v. M'Faddon* (1812)[80] in order of preference on the docket. Marshall delivered the opinion of the Court on "the very delicate and important inquiry, whether an American citizen can assert, in an American court, title to an armed national vessel, found within the waters of the United States."[81]

The *Exchange* sailed from Baltimore October 27, 1809 enroute to Spain. Under Napoleon's decree of March 23, 1810, the vessel was seized on December 10 of that year and converted into a warship. The ship was renamed *Balaou* and, while sailing from Europe to the West Indies, was forced by inclement weather into the port of Philadelphia. The papers carried by the commander of the ship identified it as owned by Napoleon. While the ship was in port on August 24, 1811, the original owners, John M'Faddon and William Greetham, libeled the vessel, claiming ownership.

Marshall found that he must explore an "unbeaten path relying on general principles," and followed the "principle of public law that national ships of war, entering the port of a friendly power open for their reception, [were] to be considered as exempted by the consent of that power from its jurisdiction."[82]

The objectivity of the decision confirming ownership in Napoleon and dismissing the libel contrasted sharply with the policy announced by Napoleon in the Continental System.

In the case of *The Nereide* (1815),[83] Marshall discussed fully the law contained in the Pinckney Treaty, emphasizing those principles which he, as Secretary of State, had urged on Humphreys. In this case, Manuel Pinto, a native of Buenos Aires with business in London, contracted with John Drinkald, master of the *Nereide*, to sail with cargo from London to Buenos Aires and back to London. She sailed under convoy from which she became detached and, on December 19, 1813, was captured, taken to New York, and condemned for prize. Pinto filed a claim on behalf of himself, his father and his sister as co-owners. Marshall decided that Pinto was a neutral who had loaded his cargo in an enemy ship. He addressed the question, "Whether the treaty between Spain and the United States subjected the goods of either party, being neutral, to condemnation as enemy property, if found by the other in the vessel of an enemy."[84] Marshall found that the parties by treaty had agreed that "free ships make free goods" and thus had ameliorated the old law. He rejected the argument, "enemy ships make enemy goods," reasoning that a neutral by placing his goods in an enemy vessel did not thereby adopt the position of the enemy. He held that the neutral goods should be returned to Pinto. Story filed a lengthy dissent arguing that "Pinto, by voluntarily sailing under convoy, forfeited his neutrality and bound his property to an indissolubly hostile character."[85]

Disputes over insurance coverage brought questions of blockade before the Court. In *Olivera v. The Union Insurance Co.* (1818),[86] the Spanish brig, *St. Francis de Assise*, on a neutral voyage from Baltimore to Havana, was stopped in the mouth of the Chesapeake Bay on February 8, 1813, by four British frigates who ordered the vessel to return to port. The brig was covered for the trip by the Union Insurance Company, which refused to pay for the loss occasioned by the abandoned shipment. In addition to usual perils, "all unlawful arrests, restraints, and detainments of all kinds" were covered by the policy. Marshall discussed the divided opinions of the various courts on whether a blockade is comprehended within the perils insured against. In the instant case, he concluded that the blockade was a restraint within the terms of the policy. He recognized the right of the belligerent to blockade the port of the enemy, but the right of the neutral vessel to leave was equally assured by international law.[87]

Insurance companies often defended that the negligence of the vessel in approaching a blockade caused the loss. On a voyage from Charleston to Cadiz, the brig *John* was captured by a blockading British force as she approached the port and was sent to Gibralter to be condemned as prize.[88] Marshall observed that the "fact of clearing out for a blockaded port is in itself innocent, unless it be accompanied with knowledge of the blockade." Relying on Vattel, he found that the right to treat the neutral vessel as an enemy arises only when the neutral vessel enters the port with knowledge that the blockade is in force. As the *John* entered without knowledge of the blockade, she was not subject to seizure and condemnation. The Court therefore considered the judgment of the vice admiralty court in Gibralter void and ordered recovery from the insurance company. Marshall consistently ruled that innocent entry to a blockaded port did not violate the law of blockade or absolve the insurance company which otherwise would be liable for the loss. He held that the approaching vessel need only make inquiry at the blockading port.

Marshall spoke on the subject of contraband in *The Commercen* (1816)[89] when the Swedish vessel was captured by the United States privateer *Lawrence*, on a voyage from Ireland to Spain with a cargo of barley and oats for the use of Britain's military forces in Spain. Sweden was neutral as to the United States but allied with Great Britain in the war on the Continent. As a neutral vessel whose rights had been violated, the *Commercen* sued for an award of freight. Justice Story, in the ruling opinion, observed that goods destined for ordinary use of life in the enemy's country were not contraband but "if destined for military use" were considered contraband,[90] and he denied the award. Marshall filed a dissent with which Justices Livingston and Johnson concurred. Marshall agreed that the goods were contraband, but he noted that Sweden was allied with Great Britain in a war against France. She had a belligerent's "right to convey military stores for the use of British armies" engaged in the war.

International disputes came before the Marshall Court, presenting problems with which Marshall, as Secretary of State, had been directly involved or presenting situations new to him but similar in substance. His nine months as Secretary of State enabled him to articulate the principles of neutrality which he applied on the Court. As Secretary, he directed negotiations conforming to the law of nations to resolve disputes through agreement. As Chief Justice, he directed settlements conforming to the law of nations when negotiations had failed.

## NOTES

1. Adams recognized, at this time, that Hamilton commanded personal loyalty from certain of his cabinet members. Historians have referred to these Federalists "committed to the Hamilton program" as High Federalists and to those "who preferred to go along with the President" as Moderate or Adams's Federalists. Hamilton's influence within the cabinet is documented in Alexander DeConde, *The Quasi-War: The Politics and Diplomacy of the Undeclared War With France, 1797-1801* (New York: Charles Scribner's Sons, 1966). New England federalists from Essex County, Massachusetts, representing the rich and well-born organized in 1778 and were referred to as the Essex junto by their opponents, notably Jefferson. They formed a conservative branch within the party. They were considered pro-British and

wanted war with France during the Adams administration. DeConde contended that the Essex junto typified the thinking of the High Federalists, but Hamilton did not favor full-scale war with France. He had an elaborate foreign policy program which included limited war efforts. *Id.*, 77, 104-5. Adams "sacrificed [his] popularity in New England," with this group, by sending the Ellsworth Mission to France. See Lester J. Cappon, *The Adams-Jefferson Letters: The Complete Correspondence Between Thomas Jefferson and Abigail and John Adams* (Chapel Hill: The University of North Carolina Press, 1959), vol. 2, p. 300, n. 49., and Adams to Jefferson, February 3, 1812, at p. 295. See also Samuel Flagg Bemis, *John Quincy Adams and the Foundations of American Foreign Policy* (New York: Alfred A. Knopf, 1949), p. 101-7.

2. Beveridge, *The Life of John Marshall*, vol. 2, pp. 157-58.

3. Stephen G. Kurtz, *The Presidency of John Adams: The Collapse of Federalism, 1795-1800* (Philadelphia: University of Pennsylvania Press, 1957), p. 390.

4. DeConde, *The Quasi-War*, p. 274. Samuel Flagg Bemis denied that the "political schism" in the Federalist Party was caused by Adam's foreign policy. It was, instead, a "cleavage between agrarianism and merchantilism within the party . . . that brought about the downfall of the Federalists." Bemis reasoned that Adams ran ahead of his party in the election in 1800, and that his foreign policy almost reelected him. See Bemis, *John Quincy Adams and the Foundations of American Foreign Policy*, pp. 106-7. Stephen Kurtz agreed with Bemis that Adams' peace policy helped him in the election. See Kurtz, *The Presidency of John Adams*, pp. 378-83.

5. For a discussion of anti-Federalist sentiment during this period, see James H. Broussard, *The Southern Federalists, 1800-1816*, (Baton Rouge: Louisiana State University Press, 1978). Broussard reported that in "early 1800 . . . public feeling shifted from fear of France to resentment of Federalism at home, and for this change President Adams' peace policy was partly responsible." *Id.* at 15.

6. John S. Adams, ed., *An Autobiographical Sketch by John Marshall . . .* (Ann Arbor, Mich.: University of Michigan Press, 1937), pp. 28-29.

7. Broussard, *The Southern Federalists*, p. 68.

8. Marshall, Secretary of State at the time of the disputed election, expressed initially a preference for Burr's election. He was convinced by Hamilton that Burr presented a greater danger, but he decided that he would not endorse either candidate because an endorsement might be interpreted as an attempt to curry favor with the candidate. Marshall also expressed in this letter to Hamilton the fact that "no consideration could induce" him to serve as Secretary of State under a "President whose political system" was "at variance" with his own. John C. Hamilton, ed., *The Works of Alexander Hamilton* (New York: J. F. Trow, Printer, 1850), vol. 2, Marshall to Hamilton, January, 1801, p. 445.

9. See generally Cullen, ed., *The Papers of John Marshall*, vol. 4, pp.

156 et seq. See also Gibbs, ed., *The Administrations of Washington and Adams*, vol. 2, pp. 348-50, where Gibbs reported the content of Adams' letters to William Cunningham. Adams responded to questions about Pickering's removal, "I could get nothing done as I would have it. My new minister, Marshall, did all to my entire satisfaction." *Id.*, at 349. Gibbs editorialized:

> With regard to Gen. Marshall's doing every thing to his entire satisfaction, Mr. Adams' simplicity is amusing enough. Every one who knew that great man, knew that he possessed to an extraordinary degree the faculty of putting his own ideas into the minds of others, unconsciously to them. The secret of Mr. Adams' satisfaction was, that he had obeyed his Secretary of State without suspecting it.

*Id.*, at 350.

10. Oliver Wolcott to Fisher Ames, August 10, 1800, Gibbs, ed., *Memoirs of the Administrations of Washington and John Adams* vol. 2, p. 402. Wolcott added that he thought Marshall would be "out of his proper element."

11. DeConde, *The Quasi-War*, p. 272.

12. Hamilton to Wolcott, December 16, 1800, Gibbs, ed., *Memoirs of the Administrations of Washington and Adams*, vol. 2, p. 458.

13. During this period, Marshall drew only the salary for the Court position. See Beveridge, *The Life of John Marshall*, vol. 2, pp. 552-59.

14. Beveridge, *The Life of John Marshall*, vol. 2, pp. 530-31. Beveridge reported that Marshall wrote two speeches in his own handwriting for Adams to deliver on December 3, 1800, to Congress. One, the better one according to Beveridge, was not delivered. He also reported that Marshall wrote two other short speeches for delivery to the House and to the Senate. *Id.*, at 531, n. 2. A speech drafted by Marshall and one "digested" by the cabinet are reproduced in Hobson, ed., *The Papers of John Marshall*, vol. 6, pp. 7-10 and pp. 11-14. The editors note that Adams delivered the revised speech on November 22, 1800 to Congress. *Id.*, at p. 10, n. 1.

15. Cullen, ed., *The Papers of John Marshall*, vol. 4, p. 160. Baker reported Marshall had a staff of nine while at the Department of State with combined salaries of $6,500. The Secretary of State salary at the time added an additional $5,000 for a total of $11,500. See Baker, *John Marshall*, p. 332.

16. From American Envoys, April 18, 1800, Cullen, ed., *The Papers of John Marshall*, vol. 4, pp. 131-32.

17. *Ibid.*, Marshall to Adams, July 21, 1800, pp. 184-85.

18. *Ibid.*, Marshall to Pickering, July 23, 1800, p. 187.

19. *Ibid.*, Adams to Marshall, July 31, 1800, pp. 194-95.

20. *Ibid.*, Marshall to Adams, August 25, 1800, p. 240.

21. *Ibid.*, Adams to Marshall, September 4, 1800, p. 256.

22. *Ibid.*, pp. 256-57. Adams referred to the Supreme Court decision of *Bas v. Tingy*, 4 Dallas 37 (1800). Justice Washington gave the unanimous

opinion of the Court. Justice Chase filed a concurring opinion. The case involved the claim of a public armed ship, *Ganges*, for salvage. *The Ganges* recaptured the *Eliza*, owned by John Bas, which had been taken at sea by French privateers. Two Congressional acts, one of June 28, 1798, and one of March 2, 1799, provided differently for salvage to be paid by the owner to the recapturing party. The second act assessed the salvage value at one-half the ship's value if the ship had been in the hands of the enemy more than ninety-six hours, as *Eliza* had. The trial and the appellate courts held that the salvage was to be predicated on the later act and the Supreme Court affirmed. To reach its decision, the Court determined that France came within the definition of enemy under the act. Washington distinguished between two types of public war, "If it be declared in form, it is called solemn, and is of the perfect kind;" and "imperfect war, . . . being limited as to places, persons, and things; because not solemn, and because those who are authorized to commit hostilities, act under special authority, and can go no farther than to the extent of their commission." *Id.*, at 40.

23. Marshall to Adams, September 17, 1800, Cullen, ed., *The Papers of John Marshall*, vol. 4, pp. 279-80.

24. *Ibid.*, From American Envoys, August 15, 1800, pp. 219-20.

25. *Ibid.*, Murray to Marshall, p. 310.

26. DeConde, *The Quasi-War*, p. 244. All of these neutral principles had been a part of the Declaration of Neutrality of 1780 proclaimed by Catherine the Great. With Napoleon's encouragement, her son, Tsar Paul I, incorporated them into his Declaration of Armed Neutrality proclaimed on August 27, 1800.

27. *Ibid*, p. 298. See also Bemis, *John Quincy Adams and the Foundations of American Foreign Policy*, pp. 90-108. Bemis recounts that Adams in 1794 had favored the idea of another armed neutrality, but his ideas changed after the Jay Treaty was signed. *Id.*, p. 92. John Quincy Adams, on January 27, 1801, wrote to William Vans Murray that the plan of a new armed neutrality first appealed to him but that he became convinced after watching Russia and Prussia that the United States policy should "have nothing to do with it." Earlier State Department correspondence reveals that Secretary of State Pickering and President Adams were also instrumental in his change of view. *Id.*, p. 93.

28. Cullen, *The Papers of John Marshall*, vol. 4, pp. 254-55.

29. *Ibid.*, p. 255, n. 2. The editors of *The Marshall Papers* note that "Napoleon's wish to conciliate the United States by terminating the Quasi-War developed from his plan to acquire an American empire. The day after the convention of Mortefontaine was signed, Berthier signed the secret treaty of Ildefonso with Spain, which exchanged a kingdom in Italy for Louisiana and 6 warships."

30. DeConde, *The Quasi-War*, pp. 303-05. Both the Adams and Jefferson administrations refused to "have any more to do with the . . . famous league [which] collapsed when the British Navy blasted Denmark out of it and

young Alexander I . . . [after assassinating his father, Paul] deserted the combination." Bemis, *John Quincy Adams*, p. 108.

31. John Quincy Adams to Marshall, June 29, 1800, Cullen, ed., *The Papers of John Marshall*, vol. 4, pp. 58-59.

32. *Ibid.*, Marshall to John Quincy Adams, pp. 188-9.

33. Ray W. Irwin, *The Diplomatic Relations of the United States with the Barbary Powers: 1776-1816* (Chapel Hill: The University of North Carolina Press, 1931), pp. 77-105. See also Gardner W. Allen, *Our Navy and the Barbary Corsairs* (New York: Houghton, Mifflin and Company, 1905).

34. Allen, *Our Navy and the Barbary Corsairs*, pp.25-42. Allen reported that "Adams and Jefferson held radically different views as to the attitude that should be assumed toward the Barbary States. The former favored a policy of peace with the payment of tribute, while Jefferson preferred war." *Id.*, at 35.

35. *Ibid.*, p. 58.

36. Marshall to Eaton, August 30, 1800, Cullen, ed., *The Papers of John Marshall*, vol. 4, p. 252.

37. *Ibid.*, Marshall to O'Brien, July 29, 1800, pp. 192-93.

38. Richard O'Brien to Secretary of State, September 20, 1800, Claude A. Swanson, ed., *Naval Documents Related to the United States Wars with the Barbary Powers* (Washington: United States Government Printing Office, 1939), vol. 1, p. 371.

39. Marshall to Griswold, January 15, 1801, Hobson, ed., *The Papers of John Marshall*, vol. 6, pp. 54-55.

40. Memoranda on Foreign Affairs [February 2, 1801], Hobson, ed., *The Papers of John Marshall*, vol. 6, pp. 65-66.

41. Allen, *Our Navy and the Barbary Corsairs*, pp. 267-301.

42. Marshall to Rufus King, September 20, 1800, Cullen, ed., *The Papers of John Marshall*, vol. 4, p. 285.

43. *Ibid.*

44. *Ibid.*, p. 288.

45. *Ibid.*, pp. 289-290.

46. *Ibid.*, pp. 291-92.

47. *Ibid.*, p. 293.

48. *Ibid.*, p. 293.

49. *Ibid.*, p. 295.

50. *Ibid.*, pp. 295-96.

51. DeConde, *The Quasi-War*, p. 201. The grievance was perhaps the single most important cause of the War of 1812, and although cessation of impressment was not made a part of the Treaty of Ghent, the practice was abandoned in the second decade of the 1800s.

52. King to Marshall, September 30, 1800, Cullen, ed., *The Papers of John Marshall*, vol. 4, p. 308.

53. Marshall to King, February 26, 1801, Hobson, ed., *The Papers of John Marshall*, vol. 6, p. 81.

54. See the full discussion of Marshall's role while Secretary of State in the British debt dispute, *supra*, ch. 2, pp. 20-23.

55. *Ibid.*, Marshall to King, August 2, 1800, p. 239. Secretary of State Pickering had submitted proposed explanatory articles to King in December of 1799.

56. *American State Papers: Foreign Relations* (Washington, D.C.: United States Government Printing Press, 1832), vol. 2, 1802, p. 389. Marshall also wrote to Samuel Sitgreaves, who was in London, to inform him that the President was ameable to Grenville's suggestion that informal explanations could be "received in lieu" of the more formal articles favored by both Marshall and Adams. *Ibid.*, Marshall to Sitgreaves, December 2, 1800, p. 388.

57. *Ibid.*

58. Marshall to King, February 26, 1801, Hobson, ed., *The Papers of John Marshall*, vol. 6, pp. 82-83.

59. King to Marshall, January 12, 1801, Hobson, ed., *The Papers of John Marshall*, vol. 6, pp. 102-103.

60. Marshall to King, May 5, 1802, Hobson, ed., *The Papers of John Marshall*, vol. 6, pp. 119-120.

61. *Ibid.*, 1801, pp. 345-47.

62. Marshall to Humphreys, September 8, 1800, Cullen, *The Papers of John Marshall*, vol. 4, p. 267.

63. *Ibid.*, p. 270.

64. *Ibid.*, p. 271.

65. *Ibid.*, pp. 272-73.

66. Marshall to Humphreys, January 5, 1801, Hobson, ed., *The Papers of John Marshall*, vol. 6, p. 50.

67. *Ibid.*, Marshall to Adams, August 30, 1800, p. 250.

68. *Ibid.*, Marshall to Adams, September 6, 1800, p. 262-63.

69. *Ibid.*, p. 263.

70. Swanson, ed., *Naval Documents Related to the Quasi-War*, vol. 6, pp. 321-22. In November, 1800, Marshall responded to a June 22 request by L'Ouverture that the president of the United States trade directly with his country. Marshall advised the new leader that the executive had no power to trade directly and that he would have to establish trade through individuals. At the same time, he assured L'Ouverture that the United States extended good will to him. Marshall to L'Ouverture, November 26, 1800, Hobson, ed., *The Papers of John Marshall*, vol. 6, p. 22.

71. The importance and popularity of Vattel in international law during this period is documented by the repeated editions that appeared after the initial publication in 1758 of his two volume work, *The Law of Nations*. During Marshall's pre-Court experience, editions were printed in 1775 in Amsterdam and in 1797 in London. In the preface to an 1833 London edition, British barrister and legal scholar Joseph Chitty noted, "It has been generally supposed that [this admirable work] is only adapted for the study of sovereigns and statesmen. . . . But it is of infinitely more extended utility . . . and . . . ought

to be studied by *every gentleman of liberal education* and by *youth*, in whom the best moral principles should be inculcated." Emmerich de Vattel, *The Law of Nations: or, Principles of the Law of Nature, applied to the Conduct and Affairs of Nations and Sovereigns* (Philadelphia: T. & J. W. Johnson, 1883), p. v. Annotated editions appeared in 1839 in Paris, and in 1852 and 1883 in Philadelphia. Nussbaum noted that translations of Vattel proliferated in the late eighteenth and first half of the nineteenth century with twenty-one French editions, twenty-three English editions of which thrirteen were American, six Spanish, one German, and one Italian. Nussbaum, *A Concise History of the Law of Nations*, p. 163.

72. Marshall to Humphreys, September 8, 1800, Cullen, ed., *The Papers of John Marshall*, vol. 4, p. 271, n. 1.

73. *Ibid.*, Marshall to King, September 20, 1800, p. 288.

74. John Marshall memoranda, February 2, 1801, RG 59, National Archives, Washington, D.C. Reproduced in Hobson, ed., *The Papers of John Marshall*, vol. 6, pp. 65-66.

75. 4 Cranch 241 (1808).

76. 4 Cranch 241, 275-76.

77. 4 Cranch 241, 272-73.

78. 4 Cranch 241, 290.

79. 4 Cranch 241, 270, 277.

80. 7 Cranch 116 (1812).

81. 7 Cranch 116, 135.

82. 7 Cranch 116, 145-46.

83. 9 Cranch 388 (1815).

84. 9 Cranch 388, 418.

85. 9 Cranch 388, 448.

86. 3 Wheaton 183 (1818).

87. 3 Wheaton 183, 195 (1818).

88. *Fitzsimmons v. The Newport Insurance Co.*, 4 Cranch 185 (1808).

89. 1 Wheaton 382 (1816).

90. 1 Wheaton 382, 388.

# 6

# Conclusion

John Marshall's contribution to establishing a firm national government with a strong judiciary overshadows his work in forging a place for the United States in the world of nations. His two contributions to the development of the American Constitution are not only consistent with but closely related to his world view. Marshall was a nationalist and a practical visionary who believed that laws effectively governing men brought happiness and order. While the separate states were defining their existence within a federal union, the nation was defining itself in the world. The Constitution provided the structure within which the states would coexist harmoniously. International law could provide the structure enabling the nations to live in peace. Marshall embraced the order offered by both, while accepting without reservation the basic concept of international law that "nations have an absolute right to self-preservation and independence."[1]

Chancellor James Kent in 1824 contended that a knowledge of international law was important to "every gentleman who [was] animated by . . . ambition to assume stations of high public trust." He described it as "elementary learning" and an "essential part of the education of an American lawyer."[2] Marshall did not systematize his concepts of international law, but his experiences in the practice of law, in international diplomacy, in Congress, in the State Department, and on the Court required a working knowledge of the rules governing nations. James Kent and another contemporary, Henry Wheaton, systematized the law that Marshall, with other jurists, was helping to create.[3]

Marshall's familiarity with the treatises of international law is evident in his arguments in the British debt cases, which depended upon knowledge of the rules governing belligerents in time of war. Asserting that Virginia was an independent sovereign at the time of the sequestration act required Marshall to discover the attributes of sovereignty and the rights and duties of belligerents regarding confiscation of enemy property. The cases also obligated him to define and interpret provisions in the Treaty of 1783 and their effect upon municipal law.

As envoy to France, Marshall had the duty to defend neutral rights to trade with the belligerent nations in Europe. Marshall accepted the general law of nations that a belligerent had an absolute right to enter neutral ships to search for contraband. Marshall appreciated that the list of contraband in the Jay Treaty accorded with the international law definition. He understood that the definition of contraband was always a subject of negotiation between treating nations and that the United States tried to negotiate for a narrow definition of contraband because it benefited commerce. He endorsed the rule that "free ships make free goods" as a law favoring neutral rights to be acquired by treaty if possible. But he accepted the rule of the law of nations in prize cases that goods of an enemy on board the ship of a friend may be taken as good prize while neutral goods, not contraband, were safe in an enemy vessel and should be restored.[4] He understood these principles first as a statesman and then on the Supreme Court.

As a representative in Congress, Marshall found the duty of the United States to deliver up fugitives not only in the Jay Treaty but also in the law of nations. He defined the jurisdiction of a nation to include punishment for offenses committed against the municipal laws of the nation on board its private and public vessels on the high seas and over its subjects wherever found. In the Nash/Robbins case, he defined piracy under the law of nations. While on the Supreme Court, he distinguished between that definition and the definition of piracy in the municipal law of the United States. His understanding of piracy was acquired during the pre-Court years and augmented during the Court years.

As Secretary of State, Marshall's instructions reveal a complete understanding of the law of nations as it applied to relationships of nations with one another at war and at peace and as neutrals. Marshall's instructions of September 20, 1800, contained the complete definition of contraband. Articles used for war were contraband, whereas articles not so used were neutral goods. The nature of articles of ambiguous use was to be determined by the circumstances controlling the use. His decisions on the Supreme Court reflect this understanding. He also defined blockade as Secretary of State, and on the Court, he insisted that the right of neutrals to trade should be restricted by belligerents only by actual blockades and proper definition of contraband.

To infer, as Ziegler did, that Marshall in 1814 was "lost . . . in the vast field of international law when he did not have the guiding hands of the more learned counsel in the profession to lead him"[5] is to misread the man and the period. An appreciation for Marshall's experiences during the Federalist administrations of Washington and Adams disproves the assertion.

Although the parties changed and the facts varied in the cases before the Court, the problems requiring analysis under the principles of international law were the same whether Marshall addressed them in the eight-year period before he became Chief Justice or during the thirty-five years he served on the Bench. The concepts, although complicated, were not that numerous or that difficult. They were grounded in justice and involved common, recurrent disputes in the international community. Marshall had a penetrating mind and he approached issues with incisive logic.[6] He was prepared for the task of applying international law to cases before he began the formal task.

Marshall, a practical man, realized that the law of nations was a response to and an alternative for the use of force in international relations. It was necessarily a practical area in the law. In responding to an interesting request in 1832, he revealed both his realistic conception of the world and his idealistic dedication to world order:

> Sir,—I have received your pamphlet proposing a Congress of Nations for the amicable adjustment of national differences, for which I thank you, together with your note requesting my opinion. I have read it with deep interest, and a sincere wish that the attainment of its object were practicable. The argument is well arranged and well supported. The quotations from the New Testament are directly applicable, and the whole spirit of the Sacred Volume inculcates peace. The human race would be eminently benefitted by the principle you advance. The religious man and the philanthropist must equally pray for its establishment. Yet I must avow my belief that it is impracticable.[7]

A century and a half later, one can only conjecture with some degree of certainty that Marshall would have been at The Hague for international peace conferences and would have wholeheartedly endorsed the growing efforts to have such a union of nations realized.

## NOTES

1. Wheaton, *Elements of International Law*, p. 101.
2. Kent, *Commentaries on American Law*, vol. 1, p. 20.
3. Wheaton observed that the law of nations could be found in "rules of conduct which ought to be observed" (discoverable through reason), in texts of scholars on international law, and in decisions of courts and boards of arbitration. Wheaton, *Elements of International Law*, p. 46-47.
4. *The Nereide*, 9 Cranch 388 (1815).
5. Ziegler, *The International Law of John Marshall*, p. 97.
6. Wheaton divided international law into two branches: (l) the natural law of nations consisting of the "rules of justice applied to the conduct of independent societies of men called States," synonymous with "international

morality" (identified also with the Law of God), and (2) the positive law of nations with its three branches, (a) voluntary law arising from usage and custom, (b) conventional law arising from treaty and convention and manifesting the express will of nations, and (c) customary law arising from the tacit consent of nations establishing a peculiar usage among certain nations. Wheaton, *Elements of International Law*, pp. 46-47.

7. *The Calumet* (November-December issue, 1832), Marshall to editor, September 12, 1832, pp. 290-91, John Marshall Papers, Manuscripts and Rare Book Department, The Earl Gregg Swem Library, The College of William and Mary, Williamsburg, Virginia.

# Bibliography


**SPECIAL COLLECTIONS**

Diplomatic Records: National Archives and Records Administration, Washington, D.C.

John Marshall Papers, Manuscript Division, Library of Congress, Washington, D.C.

John Marshall Papers, Manuscripts and Rare Books Department, Earl Gregg Swem Library, The College of William and Mary, Williamsburg, Virginia.

John Marshall Papers, Virginia Historical Society, Richmond, Virginia.

John Marshall Papers, Virginia State Library, Richmond, Virginia.

Henry Wheaton Papers, Manuscript Division, Pierpont Morgan Library, New York, New York.

**PRIMARY SOURCES PRINTED**

*American State Papers, Class I, Foreign Relations*. Vols. 1-6. Washington, D.C.: Government Printing Press, 1832.

*Annals of Congress, Sixth Congress*. Washington, D.C.: Government Printing Press, 1851.

Bartlett, Ruhl J. *The Record of American Diplomacy: Documents and Reading in the History of American Foreign Relations*. New York: Alfred A. Knopf, 1948.

Cappon, Lester J., ed. *The Adams-Jefferson Letters: The Complete Correspondence Between Thomas Jefferson and Abigail and John Adams*. Vols. 1 and 2. Chapel Hill: University of North Carolina Press, 1959.

Chinard, Gilbert, ed. *The Treaties of 1778 and Allied Documents*. Baltimore: Johns Hopkins Press, 1928.

Cullen, Charles T., ed. *The Papers of John Marshall: Correspondence and Papers, January 1799—October 1800*. Vol. 4. Chapel Hill: University of North Carolina Press, 1984.

Cullen, Charles T., and Herbert A. Johnson, ed. *The Papers of John Marshall: Correspondence and Papers, July 1788—December 1795, Account Book, July 1788—December 1795*. Vol. 2. Chapel Hill: University of North Carolina Press, 1977.

Du Ponceau, Peter Stephen, trans. *A Treatise on the Law of War by Cornelius Van Bynkershoek Being the First Book of His Quaestiones Juris Publici*. Philadelphia: Farrand & Nicolas, 1810.

Ford, Paul Leicester, ed. *The Works of Thomas Jefferson*. The Federal Edition. Vols. 1, 5, 12. New York: The Knickerbocker Press, 1904.

Gibbs, George, ed. *Memoirs of the Administrations of Washington and John Adams, Edited from the Papers of Oliver Wolcott, Secretary of the Treasury*. Vols. 1 and 2. New York: William Van Norden, Printer, 1846.

Hall, John E. *An Essay on Maritime Loans, From the French of M. Balthazard Marie Emerigon*. Baltimore: Philip H. Nicklin & Co., 1811.

Hall, John E., ed. *The American Law Journal and Miscellaneous Repertory*. Vols. 1-3. Boston: Farrand and Company, 1808-1810.

Hall, John E., ed. *The American Law Journal*. New series, Vol. 4. Philadelphia: Sergeant Hall, Printer, 1813.

Hall, John E., ed. *The American Law Journal*. Vol. 5. Baltimore: William Fry, 1814.

Hall, John E., ed. *The American Law Journal*. Vol. 6. Philadelphia: James Maxwell, Printer, 1817.

Hamilton, Stanislaus Murray, ed. *The Writings of James Monroe, Including a Collection of His Public and Private Papers and Correspondence Now for the First Time Printed: 1778-1794*. Vol. 1. New York: G. P. Putnam's Sons, 1898.

Hay, George. *A Treatise on Expatriation*. Washington, D.C.: A. & G. Way, Printers, 1814.

Hobson, Charles F., ed. *The Papers of John Marshall: Selected Law Cases, 1784-1800*. Vol. 5. Chapel Hill: University of North Carolina Press, 1987.

________. *The Papers of John Marshall: Correspondence, Papers, and Selected Judicial Opinions November 1800—March 1807.* Vol. 6. Chapel Hill: University of North Carolina Press, 1990.

Hunt, Gaillard, ed. *The Writings of James Madison: Comprising His Public Papers and His Private Correspondence, Including Numerous Letters and Documents Now for the First Time Printed, 1790-1802.* Vol. 6. New York: G. P. Putnam's Sons, 1906.

Jameson, J. Franklin, ed. *Privateering and Piracy in the Colonial Period: Illustrative Documents.* New York: Augustus M. Kelley, 1970 <1923>.

Johnson, Herbert A, ed. *The Papers of John Marshall: Correspondence and Papers, November 10, 1775—June 23, 1788, Account Book, September 1782—June 1788.* Vol. 1. Chapel Hill: University of North Carolina Press, 1974.

*Journal of the House of Delegates of the Commonwealth of Virginia, Begun and Held in the City of Richmond, in the County of Henrico.* Richmond: Thomas W. White, Opposite the Bell-Tavern, 1828.

Kent, James. *Commentaries on American Law.* New York: O. Halsted, 1827.

Kent, William, ed. *Memoirs and Letters of James Kent.* Boston: Da Capo Press, 1970 <1898>.

Lowell, John. *Mr. Madison's War: A Dispassionate Inquiry into the Reasons Alleged by Mr. Madison for Declaring an Offensive and Ruinous War Against Great Britain.* N.Y.: L. Beach, 1812.

________. *Peace Without Dishonour—War Without Hope: Being A Calm and Dispassionate Enquiry into the Question of the Chesapeake, and the Necessity and Expediency of War.* Boston: Greenough and Stebbins, 1807.

________. *Review of a Treatise on Expatriation by George Hay, Esquire.* Boston: Russell, Cutler & Co., 1814.

Malone, Dumas, ed. *Correspondence Between Thomas Jefferson and Pierre Samuel Du Pont de Nemours.* Boston: Houghton Mifflin Company, 1930.

Mason, Frances Norton. *My Dearest Polly: Letters of the Chief Justice to His Wife, 1779-1831.* Richmond: Garrett and Massie, 1961.

Marsden, Reginald Geoffrey, ed. *Documents Relating to Law and Custom of the Sea.* Vols. 1 and 2. London: Navy Records Society, 1915.

Marshall, John. *Autobiography.* John Stokes Adams, ed. *An Autobiographical Sketch of John Marshall.* Ann Arbor: University of Michigan Press, 1937.

________. *George Washington.* American Statesmen, Second Series. New York: Chelsea House, 1983 <1804, 1805, 1807>.

Moore, John Bassett. *History and Digest of the International Arbitrations to Which the United States Has Been a Party.* Vol. 1. Washington, D.C.: Government Printing Office, 1898.

Morris, Richard B., ed. *John Jay: The Winning of the Peace, Unpublished Papers, 1780—1784*. Vol. 2. New York: Harper and Row, Publishers, 1980.

Roche, John P., and Stanley B. Bernstein, eds. *John Marshall: Major Opinions and Other Writings*. New York: Bobbs-Merrill Company, Inc., 1967.

Savage, Carlton, ed. *Policy of the United Toward Maritime Commerce in War: 1776-1914*. Vol. 1. Washington, D.C.: Government Printing Office, 1934.

Schwartz, Mortimer D., and John Hogan, ed. *Joseph Story: A Collection of Writings by and about An Eminent American Jurist*. New York: Oceana Publications, Inc., 1959.

Story, William W., ed. *The Miscellaneous Writings of Joseph Story*. Boston: Charles C. Little and James Brown, 1852.

Stinchcombe, William C., and Charles T. Cullen, ed. *The Papers of John Marshall: Correspondence and Papers, January 1796—December 1798*. Vol. 3. Chapel Hill: University of North Carolina Press, 1979.

Swanson, Claude A., ed. *Naval Documents Related to the United States War with the Barbary Powers*. Washington, D.C.: Government Printing Office, 1939.

________, ed. *Naval Documents Related to the Quasi-War Between the United States and France: From June 1800 to November 1800*. Washington, D.C.: Government Printing Office, 1938.

________, ed. *Naval Documents Related to the Quasi-War Between the United States and France: From December 1800 to 1801*. Secretary of the Navy. Washington, D.C.: Government Printing Office, 1938.

Vattel, Emmerich de. *The Law of Nations: or, Principles of the Law of Nature, Applied to the Conduct and Affairs of Nations and Sovereigns*. Philadelphia: T. & J. W. Johnson & Co., 1883.

________. *The Law of Nations: or, Principles of the Law of Nature, Applied to the Conduct and Affairs of Nations and Sovereigns*. London: G. G. and J. Robinson, Paternoster-Row, 1797.

Wheaton, Henry. *A Digest of the Law of Maritime Captures*. New York: R. M'Dermut and D. D. Arden, 1815.

________. *Elements of International Law*. Philadelphia: Lea and Blanchard, 1846 <1836>.

Wirt, William. *Sketches of the Life and Character of Patrick Henry*. New York: Derby and Jackson, 1857 <1817>.

## MISCELLANEOUS

*The Aurora*, Philadelphia, Pennsylvania.

*Niles Weekly Register*, Baltimore, Maryland.

*Reports of Cases Argued and Adjudged in the Supreme Court of the United States by William Cranch*. Vols. I-IX.

*Reports of Cases Argued and Adjudged in the Supreme Court of the United States by Richard Peters*. Vols. I-IX.

*Reports of Cases Argued and Adjudged in the Supreme Court of the United States by Henry Wheaton*. Vols. I-XII.

Scott, James Brown. *The Classics of International Law*.

Bynkershoek, Cornelius van. *De dominio maris*. English transalation by Ralph Van Deman Magoffin. New York. 1923.

Gentili, Alberico. *De jure belli*. English translation by John C. Rolfe. 2 vols. Oxford, 1933.

Grotius, Hugo. *De jure belli ac pacis*. English translation by Francis W. Kelsey. 2 vols. Oxford, 1925.

Pufendorf, Samuel. *De jure naturae et gentium*. English translation by C. H. and W. A. Oldfather. 2 vols. Oxford, 1934.

Vattel, Emmerich de. *Le droit des gens*. English translation by Charles G. Fenwick. 3 vols. Washington, 1916.

*The Virginia Gazette, and General Advertiser*, Richmond, Virginia.

## CASES

*The Alexander*. 8 Cranch 169 (1814).

*American Insurance Company v. Canter*. 1 Peters 511 (1828).

*The Anna Maria*. 2 Wheaton 327 (1817).

*The Antelope*. 10 Wheaton 66 (1825).

*The Astrea*. 1 Wheaton 125 (1816).

*The Atalanta*. 3 Wheaton 409 (1818).

*Bas v. Tingy. 4 Dallas 37* (1800).

*Bright's Lessee v. Rochester*. 7 Wheaton 535 (1822).

*The Brig Short Staple and Cargo v. United States*. 9 Cranch 55 (1815).

*Brown v. United States*. 8 Cranch 110 (1814).

*Carneal v. Banks*. 10 Wheaton 181 (1825).

*Cherokee Nation v. Georgia*. 5 Peters 1 (1831).

*Chirac v. Chirac*. 2 Wheaton 259 (1817).

*Church v. Hubbard*. 2 Cranch 187 (1804).

*Delassus v. United States*. 9 Peters 117 (1835).

*Dunlop and Company v. Ball*. 2 Cranch 180 (1804).

*Fitzsimmons v. Newport Insurance Company*. 4 Cranch 185 (1808).

*Foster and Elam v. Neilson* . 2 Peters 253 (1829)

*The Frances (4 of 6 Claims)*. 8 Cranch 335 (1814).

*The Friendschaft*. 3 Wheaton 14 (1808).

*The George*. 1 Wheaton 408 (1816).
*The Gran Para*. 7 Wheaton 471 (1822).
*The Grotius*. 8 Cranch 456 (1814).
*Hallet v. Jenks*. 3 Cranch 210 (1805).
*Handly's Lessee v. Anthony*. 5 Wheaton 374 (1820).
*Hannay v. Eve*. 3 Cranch 242 (1806).
*Henderson v. Poindexter's Lessee*. 12 Wheaton 530 (1827).
*Higginson v. Mein*. 4 Cranch 415 (1808).
*The Hiram*. 1 Wheaton 440 (1816).
*Hopkirk v. Bell*. 3 Cranch 454 (1806).
*The Commercen*. 1 Wheaton 382 (1816).
*Hudson v. Guestier*. 4 Cranch 293 (1808).
*Johnson and Graham's Lessee v. M'Intosh*. 8 Wheaton 543 (1823).
*Jones v. Walker*. U.S. Circuit Court, Va., Ended Cases (Restored) (1797).
*Little v. Barreme*. 2 Cranch 170 (1804).
*Livingston v. Maryland Insurance Company*. 7 Cranch 506 (1813).
*Maley v. Shattuck*. 3 Cranch 458 (1806).
*Martin v. Hunter's Lessee*. 1 Wheaton 304 (1816).
*The Mary and Susan*. 1 Wheaton 25 (1816).
*Maryland Insurance Company v. Woods*. 6 Cranch 29 (1810).
*The Mary*. 9 Cranch 126 (1815).
*The Merrimack (3 of 4 Claims)*. 8 Cranch 317 (1814).
*The Monte Allegre*. 7 Wheaton 520 (1822).
*Murray v. Schooner Charming Betsey*. 2 Cranch 64 (1804).
*The Nereide*. 9 Cranch 388 (1815).
*The Nereid*. 1 Wheaton 171 (1816).
*New Orleans, Mayor of v. DeArmas*. 9 Peters 224 (1835).
*Olivera v. Union Insurance Company*. 3 Wheaton 183 (1818).
*Owings v. Norwood's Lessee*. 5 Cranch 344 (1809).
*Patton v. Nicholson*. 3 Wheaton 204 (1818).
*Rose v. Himely*. 4 Cranch 241 (1808).
*Sands v. Knox*. 3 Cranch 499 (1806).
*Schooner Exchange v. M'Faddon*. 7 Cranch 116 (1812).
*The Ship Richmond v. United States*. 9 Cranch 102 (1815).
*The Societe*. 9 Cranch 209 (1815).
*Soulard v. United States*. 4 Peters 511 (1830).
*Talbot v. Seeman*. 1 Cranch 1 (1801).
*Thirty Hogsheads of Sugar v. Boyle*. 9 Cranch 191 (1815).
*United States v. Clarke*. 8 Peters 436 (1834).
*United States v. Klintock*. 5 Wheaton 144 (1820).
*United States v. Palmer*. 3 Wheaton 610 (1818).
*United States v. Percheman*. 7 Peters 51 (1833).
*United States v. Schooner Betsy and Charlotte*. 4 Cranch 443 (1808).
*United States v. Schooner Peggy*. 1 Cranch 103 (1801).
*United States v. Soulard*. 4 Peters 511 (1830).

*The Venus*. 8 Cranch 253 (1814).
*Ware v. Hylton*. 3 Dallas 199 (1796).
*Worcester v. Georgia*. 6 Peters 515 (1832).
*Yeaton v. Fry*. 5 Cranch 335 (1809).

## SECONDARY SOURCES

Adams, Randolph Greenfield. *A History of the Foreign Policy of the United States*. New York: The Macmillan Company, 1924.

Allen, Gardner W. *Our Naval War with France*. New York: Houghton Mifflin Company, 1909.

________. *Our Navy and the Barbary Corsairs*. New York: Houghton, Mifflin and Company, 1905.

Ammon, Harry. *The Genet Mission*. New York: W. W. Norton and Company, 1973.

Anderson, Dice Robins. "Edmund Randolph." In *The American Secretaries of State and Their Diplomacy*, ed. Samuel Flagg Bemis. Vol. 2. New York: Alfred A. Knopf, 1927.

Baker, Leonard. *John Marshall: A Life in Law*. New York: Macmillan Publishing Co., Inc., 1974.

Bar-Yaacov, Nissim. *Dual Nationality*. New York: Frederick A. Praeger, 1961.

Beeman, Richard R. *The Old Dominion and the New Nation*. Lexington: University Press of Kentucky, 1972.

Bemis, George. *Precedents of American Neutrality: In Reply to the Speech of Sir Roundell Palmer, Attorney-General of England, in the British House of Commons, May 13, 1864*. Boston: Little, Brown and Company, 1864.

Bemis, Samuel Flagg. *Jay's Treaty: A Study in Commerce and Diplomacy*. New York: The Macmillan Company, 1923.

________. *John Quincy Adams and the Foundations of American Foreign Policy*. New York: Alfred A. Knopf, 1949.

________. "Thomas Jefferson" In *The American Secretaries of State and Their Diplomacy*, ed. Samuel Flagg Bemis. New York: Alfred A. Knopf, 1927.

Beveridge, Albert J. *The Life of John Marshall: Conflict and Construction, 1800-1815*. Vol. 3. Dunwoody, Ga.: Norman S. Berg, Publisher, 1974 <1919>.

________. *The Life of John Marshall: Frontiersman, Soldier, Lawmaker 1755-1788*. Vol. 1. Dunwoody, Ga.: Norman S. Berg, Publisher, 1974.

________. *The Life of John Marshall: Politician, Diplomatist, Statesman, 1789-1801*. Vol. 2. Dunwoody, Ga.: Norman S. Berg, Publisher, 1974.

________. *The Life of John Marshall: The Building of the Nation*. Vol. 4. Dunwoody, Ga.: Norman S. Berg, Publisher, 1974 <1919>.

Binney, Horace. *An Eulogy on the Life and Character of John Marshall, Chief Justice of the Supreme Court of the United States*. Philadelphia: J. Crissy and G. Goodman, 1935.

Bourguignon, Henry J. *The First Federal Appellate Prize Court of the American Revolution, 1775-1787*. Memoirs of the American Philosophical Society for Promoting Useful Knowledge. 122. Philadelphia: The American Philosophical Society, 1977.

________. *Sir William Scott, Lord Stowell: Judge of the High Court of Admiralty, 1798-1828*. Cambridge: Cambridge University Press, 1987.

Broussard, James H. *The Southern Federalists, 1800-1816*. Baton Rouge: Louisiana State University Press, 1978.

Butler, Sir Geoffrey, and Simon Maccoby. *The Development of International Law*. London: Longmans, Green and Co. Ltd., 1928.

Chumbley, George Lewis. *Colonial Justice in Virginia*. Richmond, Va.: The Dietz Press, 1938.

Cooke, Jacob Ernest. *Alexander Hamilton*. New York: Charles Scribner's Sons, 1982.

Corbett, Percy E. *Law in Diplomacy*. Princeton: Princeton University Press, 1959.

________. *Law and Society in the Relations of States*. New York: Harcourt, Brace and Company, 1951.

________. *The Study of International Law*. New York: Doubleday and Company, Inc., 1955.

Craigmyle, Lord. *John Marshall in Diplomacy and Law*. New York, 1933.

DeConde, Alexander. *Entangling Alliance: Politics and Diplomacy under George Washington*. Durham, N.C.: Duke University Press, 1958.

________. *A History of American Foreign Policy: Growth to World Power (1700-1914)*. Vol. 1. New York: Charles Scribner's Sons, New York.

________. *The Quasi-War: The Politics and Diplomacy of the Undeclared War with France, 1797-1801*. New York: Charles Scribner's Sons, 1966.

________. *This Affair of Louisiana*. New York: Charles Scribner's Sons, 1976.

Dill, Alonzo Thomas. *George Wythe: Teacher of Liberty*. Williamsburg, Va: Virginia Independence Bicentennial Commission, 1979.

Dull, Jonathan R. *A Diplomatic History of the American Revolution*. New Haven: Yale University Press, 1985.

Dumbauld, Edward. *Thomas Jefferson and the Law*. Norman: University of Oklahoma Press, 1978.

Dunne, Gerald T. *Justice Joseph Story and the Rise of the Supreme Court.* New York: Simon and Schuster, 1969.

Fenwick, Charles G. *American Neutrality: Trial and Failure.* New York: New York University Press, 1940.

Ferrell, Robert H. *American Diplomacy, A History.* New York: W. W. Norton & Co., Inc., 1975.

Ford, Henry J. "Timothy Pickering." In *The American Secretaries of State and Their Diplomacy*, ed. Samuel Flagg Bemis. New York: Alfred A. Knopf, Inc., 1927.

Gilbert, Daniel R. *John Marshall and the Development of a National History.* In *The Colonial Legacy: Historians of Nature and Man's Nature*, ed. Lawrence H. Leder. Early Nationalist Historians Vol. 4. New York, Harper and Row, Publishers.

Gilmore, James H. *Notes of a Course of Lectures on Vattel's Law of Nations.* James Blakey, Publisher, 1891.

Goebel, Jr., Julius. *Antecedents and Beginnings to 1801.* The Oliver Wendell Holmes Devise History of the Supreme Court of the United States. Vol. 1. New York: The Macmillan Company, 1971.

Haskins, George Lee, and Herbert A. Johnson. *Foundations of Power: John Marshall, 1801-15.* The Oliver Wendell Holmes Devise History of the Supreme Court of the United States. Vol. 2. New York: Macmillan Publishing Co., Inc., 1981.

Hill, Charles E. *Leading American Treaties.* New York: AMS Press, Inc., 1969 <1922>.

Hurst, James Willard. *The Growth of American Law.* Boston: Little, Brown and Company, 1950.

Hyde, Charles Cheney. *International Law Chiefly as Interpreted and Applied by the United States.* Vols. 1 and 2. Boston: Little, Brown, and Company, 1922.

Irwin, Ray W. *The Diplomatic Relations of the United States with the Barbary Powers, 1776-1816.* Chapel Hill: University of North Carolina Press, 1931.

Jessup, Philip C., ed. *Essays on International Law from the Columbia Law Review.* New York: Columbia Law Review Association, 1965.

Jessup, Philip C., and Francis Deak. *Neutrality: Its History, Economics and Law.* Vols. 1 and 2. New York: Columbia University Press, 1935.

Jordan, Daniel P. *Political Leadership in Jefferson's Virginia.* Charlottesville, Va.: University Press of Virginia, 1983.

Konefsky, Samuel J. *John Marshall and Alexander Hamilton: Architects of the American Constitution.* New York: The Macmillan Company, 1964.

Kurtz, Stephen G. *The Presidency of John Adams: The Collapse of Federalism, 1795-1800.* Philadelphia: University of Pennsylvania Press, 1957.

Kutler, Stanley I., ed. *John Marshall.* Great Lives Observed. Englewood Cliffs, N.J.: Prentice-Hall, Inc., 1972.

Lewis, William Draper. "John Marshall." In *Great American Lawyers: A History of the Legal Profession in America*, Ed. William Draper Lewis. 2. Philadelphia: The John C. Winston Co., 1907.

Lycan, Gilbert L. *Alexander Hamilton and American Foreign Policy: A Design for Greatness*. Norman: University of Oklahoma Press, 1970.

Magruder, Allan B. *John Marshall*. American Statesmen First Series. Boston: The Riverside Press, 1885.

Mahan, Alfred T. *Sea Power in Its Relations to the War of 1812*. 1. London: Sampson Low, Marston and Company, Ltd., 1905.

Meade, Robert Douthat. *Patrick Henry, Practical Revolutionary*. Philadelphis: J. B. Lippincott Company, 1969.

Montague, Andrew J. "John Marshall." In *The American Secretaries of State and Their Diplomacy*, ed. Samuel Flagg Bemis. Vol. 2. New York: Alfred A. Knopf, Inc., 1927.

Moore, John Bassett. *International Adjudications: Ancient and Modern History and Documents*. Vols. 3, 4. New York: Oxford University Press, 1931.

________. *The Principles of American Diplomacy*. New York: Harper and Brothers Publishers, 1918 <1905>.

Morris, Richard B. *John Jay, The Nation and the Court*. Boston: Boston University Press, 1967.

________. *The Peacemakers: The Great Powers and American Independence*. New York: Harper and Row, Publishers, 1965.

Nussbaum, Arthur. *A Concise History of the Law of Nations*. New York: The Macmillan Company, 1954.

Oppenheim, L. *International Law, A Treatise*. Vols. 1 and 2. New York: Longmans, Green, and Co., 1905.

Oster, John Edward. *The Political and Economic Doctrines of John Marshall*. New York, 1967.

Pares, Richard. *Colonial Blockade and Neutral Rights, 1739-1763*. Oxford: Clarendon Press, 1938.

Pergler, Charles. *Judicial Interpretation of International Law in the United States*. New York: Macmillan Company, 1928.

Pyke, H. Reason. *The Law of Contraband of War*. Oxford: Clarendon Press, 1915.

Ralston, Jackson H. *International Arbitration from Athens to Locarno*. Stanford University: Stanford University Press, 1929.

Rhodes, Irwin S. *The Papers of John Marshall: A Descriptive Calendar*. Norman: University of Oklahoma Press, 1969.

Risjord, Norman K. *Chesapeake Politics: A Study of Maryland, Virginia and North Carolina after the Revolution*. New York: Columbia University Press, 1978.

Rose, Lisle A. *Prologue to Democracy: The Federalists in the South, 1789-1800*. Lexington: University of Kentucky Press, 1968.

Ruddy, Francis Stephen. *International Law in the Enlightenment: The Background of Emmerich de Vattel's Le Droit des Gens*. Dobbs Ferry, N.Y.: Oceana Publications, Inc., 1975.

Santvoord, G. Van. *Sketches of the Lives and Judicial Services of the Supreme Court of the United States*. N.Y.: Charles Scribner, 1854.

Seckler-Hudson, Catheryn. *Statelessness: With Special Reference to the United States*. Washington, D.C.: Digest Press, 1934.

Schuschnigg, Kurt von. *International Law: An Introduction to the Law of Peace*. Milwaukee: Bruce Publishing Company, 1959.

Schwarzenberger, Georg. *The Frontiers of International Law*. London: Stevens & Sons Ltd., 1962.

Shevory, Thomas C., ed. *John Marshall's Achievement: Law, Politics, and Constitutional Interpretations*. New York: Greenwood Press, 1989.

Smith, Herbert Arthur. *The American Supreme Court as an International Tribunal.* Germany: Wilhelm Weihert, 1977 <1922>

________. *The Law and Custom of the Sea*. New York: Frederick A. Praeger, Inc., 1950.

Smith, Sir Frederick. *The Destruction of Merchant Ships under International Law*. London: J. M. Dent & Sons, Ltd., 1917.

Stinchcombe, William. *The XYZ Affair*. Contributions in American History, Number 89. Westport, Conn.: Greenwood Press, 1980.

Swift, Richard N. *International Law: Current and Classic*. New York: John Wiley & Sons, Inc., 1969.

Stites, Francis N. *John Marshall: Defender of the Constitution*. Boston: Little, Brown and Company, 1981.

Thayer, James Bradley. *John Marshall, An Essay*. Cambridge: Cambridge University Press, 1901.

Umbreit, Kenneth Bernard. *Our Eleven Chief Justices: A History of the Supreme Court in Terms of Their Personalities*. New York: Harper and Row, 1938.

Vollenhoven, Cornelis van. *Three Stages in the Evolution of the Law of Nations*. The Hague: Martinus Nijhoff, 1919.

Walker, Thomas Alfred. *A History of the Law of Nations: From the Earliest Times to the Peace of Westphalia, 1648*. Cambridge: Cambridge University Press, 1899.

Ward, Robert. *An Enquiry into the Foundation and History of the Law of Nations in Europe from the Time of the Greeks to the Age of Grotius*. Vols. 1 and 2. Dublin: P. Wogan, P. Byrne, W. Jones and J. Rice, 1795.

Warren, Charles. *The Supreme Court in United States History: 1789-1835*. . Boston: Little, Brown and Company, 1926 <1922>.

Weis, P. *Nationality and Statelessness in International Law*. London: Stevens & Sons Ltd., 1956.

White, G. Edward. *The Marshall Court and Cultural Change, 1815-1835*. The Oliver Wendell Holmes Devise History of the Supreme Court of the United States. Vols. 3 and 4. New York: Macmillan Publishing Company, 1988.

Wolf, John B. *The Barbary Coast: Algiers Under the Turks, 1500-1830.* New York: W. W. Norton & Company, 1979.

Ziegler, Benjamin Munn. *The International Law of John Marshall.* Chapel Hill: The University of North Carolina Press, 1939.

## ARTICLES

Ammon, Harry. "Agricola Versus Aristides: James Monroe, John Marshall and the Genet Affair in Virginia." *Virginia Magazine of History and Biography* 74 (July 1966): 312-20.

Burton, Harold H. "John Marshall—The Man." *University of Pennsylvania Law Review* 104 (October 1955): 3-8.

Corwin, Edward S. "John Marshall, Malgre Lui." *University of Pennsylvania Law Review* 104 (October 1955): 9-22.

Cullen, Charles T. "New Light on John Marshall's Legal Education and Admission to the Bar." *American Journal of Legal History* 16 (1972): 345-351.

Dodd, William E. "Chief Justice Marshall and Virginia, 1813-1821." *The American Historical Review* 12 (April 1907): 776-87.

Dumbauld, Edward. "John Marshall and the Law of Nations." *University of Pennsylvania Law Review* 104 (October 1955): 38-56.

________. "John Marshall and Treaty Law." *American Journal of International Law* 50 (1956): 69-80.

Evans, Emory G. "Private Indebtedness and the Revolution in Virginia, 1776-1796." *The William and Mary Quarterly* 28 (1971 1971): 373.

Haskins, Geroge L. "John Marshall and the Commerce Clause of the Constitution." *University of Pennsylvania Law Review* 104 (October 1955): 23.

Hobson, Charles F. "The Recovery of British Debts in the Federal Circuit Court of Virginia, 1790-1797." *Virginia Magazine of History and Biography* 92 (April 1984): 176-200.

________."The Indebtedness of John Marshall to Alexander Hamilton." *Massachusetts Historical Society Proceedings* 46 (May 1913): 412-26.

Marsh, Philip. "James Monroe as `Agricola' in the Genet Controversy." *Virginia Magazine of History and Biography* 62 (October 1954): 472-76.

Marshall, Sallie Ewing. "Chief Justice John Marshall." *Magazine of American History* 12 (July-December 1884): 62-71.

Ramage, B. J. "John Marshall, Southern Federalist." *The Sewanee Review* 12 (April 1901): 129-55.

Rhodes, Irwin S. "John Marshall and the Western Country, Early Days." *Historical and Philosophical Society of Ohio Bulletin* 18 (April 1960).

Stinchcombe, William. "The Diplomacy of the WXYZ Affair." *The William and Mary Quarterly* 34 (October 1977): 590-617.

________. "Talleyrand and the American Negotiations of 1797-1798." *Journal of American History* 62 (December 1975): 575-90.

Umbanhowar, Charles Edward. "Marshall on Judging." *American Journal of Legal History* 7 (1963): 210-227.

# Index

## About the Author

FRANCES HOWELL RUDKO, an attorney in private practice for eighteen years in Fayetteville, Arkansas, is the author of *Truman's Court: A Study in Judicial Restraint* (Greenwood Press, 1988).